Dante's *Divine Comedy*
Part I

Professor William R. Cook
Professor Ronald B. Herzman

THE TEACHING COMPANY ®

PUBLISHED BY:

THE TEACHING COMPANY
4840 Westfields Boulevard, Suite 500
Chantilly, Virginia 20151-2299
1-800-TEACH-12
Fax—703-378-3819
www.teach12.com

ISBN 1-56585-859-X

William R. Cook, Ph.D.

Professor of History, State University of New York at Geneseo

William R. Cook was born and raised in Indianapolis, Indiana, and attended public schools there. He is a 1966 graduate of Wabash College in Crawfordsville, Indiana (cum laude, Phi Beta Kappa). He received Woodrow Wilson and Herbert Lehman fellowships to study Medieval History from Cornell University, where he received his Ph.D. in 1971. Professor Cook's dissertation was a study of a Hussite theologian and diplomat named Peter Payne.

In 1970, Professor Cook was appointed Assistant Professor of History at the State University of New York at Geneseo. He has taught there for 30 years and holds the rank of Distinguished Teaching Professor. SUNY Geneseo is an undergraduate college of about 5,000 students located in a village of 8,000 in the western part of New York's Finger Lakes region and about 25 miles south of Rochester.

At Geneseo, Professor Cook has taught courses in medieval history and in ancient history, the Renaissance and Reformation periods, and biblical and Christian thought. He has teamed with Professor Herzman to teach several courses, including the Age of Dante and the Age of St. Francis of Assisi.

Beginning in 1974, Professor Cook and Professor Herzman have taken their students from SUNY Geneseo to study in Europe. Recently, Professor Cook has been teaching a course about medieval Italian city-states every other January in Siena, Italy.

After publishing several articles on Hussite theology and monastic thought, Professor Cook has, for more than 20 years, focused his research on Saint Francis of Assisi. In 1989, he published a volume in a series, *The Way of the Christian Mystics*, entitled *Francis of Assisi: The Way of Poverty and Humility* with Michael Glazier (later published by the Liturgical Press, Collegeville, MN). For years, Professor Cook sought to find and catalogue all the early paintings of Saint Francis done in Italy. In the 1990s, he published a series of articles in Franciscan and Italian journals on specific images of the saint. In 1998, he published a study entitled *St. Francis in America* (Franciscan Press, Quincy, IL) of early Italian paintings of Francis that are currently in the United States and Canada. These years of research on the images of Francis were brought to a conclusion with the 1999 publication of a comprehensive catalogue: *Images of St. Francis of Assisi in Painting, Stone and Glass from the Earliest Images to ca.1320 in Italy: A Catalogue* (Leo S. Olschki, Florence) in the series *Italian Medieval and Renaissance Studies*.

Professor Cook and Professor Herzman published *The Medieval World View* with Oxford University Press in 1983 and are currently preparing a second edition. They have also written several articles together on such subjects as Dante, the *Song of Roland*, and paintings of the life of Saint Francis in Assisi.

Currently, Professor Cook is writing articles based on research that was not used in his books, and he plans to bring two great loves— Saint Francis and the city of Siena—together by doing research on the fifteenth-century Franciscan Bernardino of Siena.

Professor Cook has taught about Francis at Siena College (Loudenville, NY) and has given lectures about Francis and Franciscan art throughout the United States. With Herzman, he has taught about Francis to groups ranging from school children to students in religious education classes to Trappist monks.

Professor Cook has directed ten Seminars for School Teachers for the National Endowment for the Humanities since 1983; six have had Francis as their subject and have been conducted in Siena and Assisi, Italy.

Ronald B. Herzman, Ph.D.

Professor of English, State University of New York at Geneseo

Ronald Herzman was born in Brooklyn, New York. He attended Brooklyn Prep and Manhattan College, graduating with honor in 1965 and receiving the Devlin Medal for excellence in French. He studied English literature at the University of Delaware as a DuPont Fellow and a New York State Regents Fellow. He received his M.A. in 1967 and his Ph.D. in 1969, writing his dissertation on Geoffrey Chaucer. Professor Herzman has also studied at Princeton University (summer 1973) and as a National Endowment for the Humanities Fellow-in-Residence at the University of Chicago during the 1978–1979 academic year. He received the Chancellor's Award for Excellence in Teaching in 1976 and was awarded an honorary Doctor of Humane Letters from Manhattan College in 1991.

In 1969, Professor Herzman was appointed Assistant Professor of English at the State University of New York at Geneseo. He currently holds the rank of SUNY Distinguished Teaching Professor of English. He has held a number of concurrent positions. He has been an adjunct Professor at Genesee Community College, teaching in the inmate education program at Attica Correctional Facility (together with Professor Cook); he has been a professorial lecturer at Georgetown University; and a guest tutor at St. John's College in Santa Fe, New Mexico. From 1982–1985, Professor Herzman was on leave from SUNY to work at the National Endowment for the Humanities, where he was the founding Program Officer for the Summer Seminars for School Teachers and the Assistant Director of the Division of Fellowships and Seminars.

Professor Herzman's teaching interests include Dante, Chaucer, Francis of Assisi, Shakespeare, the Bible, and Arthurian literature. With Cook, he has team-taught several courses during the length of their academic careers at Geneseo, including the Age of Dante and the Age of St. Francis of Assisi. Professor Cook and Professor Herzman have also taken students to Europe to study various aspects of the Middle Ages.

In 1983, Professor Cook and Professor Herzman published *The Medieval World View* with Oxford University Press and are currently at work on a second edition. Professor Herzman's other books include *The Apocalyptic Imagination in Medieval Literature*

(University of Pennsylvania Press, 1992, with Richard Emmerson) and *Four Romances of England* (Medieval Institute Publications, edited with Graham Drake and Eve Salisbury). He has written extensively on medieval literature, including 15 articles and book chapters on Dante, several articles on Francis of Assisi, and work on Chaucer, the *Romance of the Rose*, and the *Song of Roland* (with Professor Cook). His current research interests include a book-length study of Dante's Paradiso.

Professor Herzman has directed nine Seminars for School Teachers for the National Endowment for the Humanities, conducted at Geneseo; at St. John's College in Santa Fe, New Mexico; and in Siena and Assisi, Italy.

Table of Contents
Dante's *Divine Comedy*
Part I

Textual quotations from Dante Alighieri's *Divine Comedy*, translated by Mark Musa, copyright © 1971 by Indiana University Press. Reproduced with permission of the publisher, Indiana University Press, Bloomington, Indiana, www.indiana.edu/~iupress.

Dante's *Divine Comedy*

Scope:

This 24-lecture course is intended to help you analyze and appreciate the long poem by Dante Alighieri (1265–1321) known as the *Divine Comedy*.

One of the most profound and satisfying poems ever written, the *Divine Comedy* (or simply the *Commedia*, to use Dante's own title) is well worth our continuing study. In its unified narrative structure, Dante incorporates aspects of the biblical and classical traditions, weaving these together in a brilliant synthesis that has helped form the basis for Western writers ever since. Or, as James Joyce once put it, "Dante is my spiritual food!"

The full achievement of the *Commedia*, however, goes far beyond anything merely structural or "literary" in a technical sense. Dante is a geographer of the cosmos, and of the individual human soul. He dramatizes and asks us to reflect on fundamental questions—questions about our political institutions and problems, the nature of our moral actions, the possibilities for spiritual transformation, and the reasons for reading and writing; questions whose poignancy the lapse of seven centuries has blunted not at all.

Dante does all this, moreover, in a demanding Italian verse form called *terza rima* and uses a complex arrangement of materials that makes the *Commedia* one of the great virtuoso pieces of world literature and most impressive artworks ever created in any medium.

The *Commedia* is a three-part journey undertaken by the pilgrim Dante to the realms of the Christian afterlife: Hell, Purgatory, and Heaven (in Italian, Inferno, Purgatorio, and Paradiso). Set at Eastertide in the year 1300, the poem begins with Dante lost midlife in a dark wood (*selva oscura*) of error. Unable to recover his true path or extricate himself from danger, he is rescued by the great Roman poet Virgil. Virgil conducts Dante first on a descent through the nine circles of hell, continues with the climbing of the seven terraces of the mount of purgatory, then directs (but does not accompany) Dante on a journey toward a personal encounter with God at the very summit of paradise.

Along the way, Dante changes guides. Virgil gives way to Beatrice, a young woman about whom Dante wrote in his early love poetry and who becomes his guide through most of the spheres of paradise. Beatrice in turn gives way to Bernard of Clairvaux, a Christian mystic who is Dante's guide for the final cantos of the Paradiso.

To explore this poem in a way that does justice to its coherence and artistic complexity, as well as to Dante's vision of the universe, we begin with a brief overview of the poem itself, then move to some of the biographical and political facts—"Dante's life and times," if you will—that you need to know to understand the poem. From there, in Lectures Three and Four, we discuss the literary texts from the biblical and classical traditions that Dante drew on in forming the *Commedia*, as well as his own early works, which were also important in shaping the poem.

We devote approximately the same number of lectures to each of the three parts of the poem, seven lectures to Inferno, six to Purgatorio, and seven to Paradiso. Because much of the poem consists of direct dramatic encounters between the pilgrim and inhabitants of the afterlife, our discussion centers primarily on these encounters. In the Inferno, these encounters are concerned with deepening Dante's (and the reader's) intellectual understanding of the nature of sin. Sin is divided into three broad categories in the *Commedia*—incontinence (subjecting reason to desire), violence, and fraud—and Lectures Six through Eleven show Dante meeting sinners drawn from each of these categories, ending with the vision of Satan frozen at the bottom of hell in Inferno 34.

In Purgatory, we see the nature and purpose of moral improvement as repentant sinners prepare themselves for the vision of God in heaven, strengthening their wills against the seven deadly sins. After spending time in antepurgatory in Lectures Twelve and Thirteen, where we learn the rules of purgatory and the nature of salvation along with the pilgrim, we move on to the terraces of purgatory proper for Lectures Fourteen through Sixteen, where we encounter the process of improvement for both Dante and those he meets there. At the end of Purgatory, in Lecture Seventeen, we are with Dante in the earthly paradise, a kind of reconstructed Garden of Eden.

In Paradiso, we journey through the created universe as seen and understood in the Middle Ages, traveling through the seven planets (as they were then understood): the moon, Mercury, Venus, the sun, Mars, Jupiter, and Saturn. Lectures Eighteen through Twenty-One deal with this journey and include memorable encounters in the

Circle of the Sun with great Christian thinkers and in the Circle of Mars with Dante's own great-great-grandfather.

In the final cantos of Paradiso, we journey through the fixed stars, then move beyond space and time as we come closer to God himself. Lecture Twenty-Two shows Dante examined by Saints Peter, James, and John on what he has learned. Lecture Twenty-Three shows Dante receiving Bernard, his final guide. Our final lecture, "In My End Is My Beginning," shows Dante in his mystical, ineffable vision of God, which brings full circle the journey that began when God's love, mediated by prayer, first sent Virgil to meet a troubled pilgrim who found himself lost "in the middle of our life's way" amid error's darkling wood.

Throughout, we will show how each part of the poem is connected to what has come before and how the questions with which Dante begins the poem are raised at ever-deeper levels of development as the journey continues. By the time your own journey through these lectures is through, we will have shown you why Dante's pilgrimage can continue to be an exceedingly enriching experience for anyone who chooses to journey along with him.

Lecture One
Reading the Poem—Issues and Editions

Scope:

This lecture introduces the entire course by outlining Dante's *Commedia* (or *Divine Comedy*, as it is often called), examining the question of translations, and providing an overview of Dante's life. The *Commedia* is one of the most impressive poems ever written, and a brief account of what the poem is about will help orient us to the nature of its achievement. The three-part journey to the realms of the Christian afterlife is impressive, both for its complexity and its interconnectedness. Because the poem is autobiographical—it is the journey of a pilgrim traveler named "Dante"—we also give a brief biographical account of Dante's life as it relates to the poem, focusing on his exile from his native Florence during the last nineteen years of his life.

Outline

I. The reader's journey into Dante's epic poem begins with a brief overview and discussion of the poem's structure.

    A. It is a remarkable, indeed unmatched, literary achievement from any point of view.

    B. It is a journey to the three parts of the Christian afterlife: hell, purgatory, and heaven, giving the afterlife a huge scope.

        1. It is cosmic in scale: Dante travels through the entire universe, from the deepest, coldest pit of hell to the very summit of heaven, where God dwells in endless glory.

        2. It addresses human concerns and questions that are valid for all times, issues of our day as well as Dante's. Among these are:

            a. What is justice?

            b. How should we be governed?

            c. What does spiritual transformation mean?

            d. Why write or read poetry? What is *any* art *for?*

    C. More than 14,000 lines long, in a very demanding verse form, it is a stylistic tour de force.

    D. Its various subdivisions give some hint of its complexity.

E. Its complexity is also figured by the significant number of dramatic encounters between the hero, Dante, and the inhabitants of the afterlife.

F. Though it is possible, when reading the poem, to "just jump in," it is probably better for the reader to approach the work armed with some background about Dante's life and times.

II. Because the poem is written in Italian, we need to say a few words about translation.

    A. Dante's poem is especially difficult to translate because of the intricate rhyme scheme, called *terza rima.*

    B. The 100 cantos (literally, "songs") average 140 lines each and are made up of three-line units called tercets.

    C. Rhyming is easier in Italian, because almost all the words end in vowels, thus giving the poet more words that rhyme with each other.

    D. Because the rhyming resources of English are relatively limited, most modern English translations do not try to imitate this form.

III. Dante scholars disagree among themselves over which is the best translation to use.

    A. Some good translations (Hollander and Durling/Martinez, for example) are not yet complete.

    B. What are the values of each of the accessible complete editions?

        1. Ciardi has a poet's sensibility.

        2. Mandelbaum provides a dual language format in an inexpensive edition.

        3. Singleton gives a fairly literal prose translation with prodigious notes.

            a. His is the scholar's choice for an English edition.

            b. It might not be the most useful edition for the non-scholar, because the notes can be overwhelming.

        4. Musa has the most useful notes and is the edition we will use here.

IV. Understanding something of Dante's own life is extremely helpful in accessing the poem.

    A. In a break with earlier epic poems, Dante casts himself as the "hero" of his own poem.

    B. His biography is, therefore, not simply window dressing, but an essential element of the poem.

    C. Dante sets the poem "halfway" through his life, in the year 1300.

V. Dante's life connects in important ways with the structure of the poem

    A. He was born in Florence in 1265.

    B. His family came from the merchant class.

    C. He was involved in the political life of his native city.

    D. He knew success as a Florentine politician and statesman but ended his life with two decades of involuntary exile.

    E. He wrote love poetry as a young man.

    F. The climax of this "youthful" poetic career was the *Vita Nuova*, an intricate combination of poems and commentary in honor of a woman named Beatrice.

    G. Dante wrote much of the *Commedia* while in exile and died in Ravenna, where he remains buried, even though Florence built him a grand tomb in the nineteenth century.

Readings:

Rachel Jacoff, ed. *The Cambridge Companion to Dante*, "The Life of Dante."

Questions to Consider:

1. Why is Dante so concerned with precise structures in his poem, and how does the intricate structure aid him in his task of writing a poem of such depth and breadth?

2. How does my reading of the poem depend at least in part on the quality and type of translation that I use?

Lecture One—Transcript
Reading the Poem—Issues and Editions

Herzman: In this first lecture, we thought we'd introduce you to Dante and to his wonderful poem the *Divine Comedy*, first, I guess, by talking just a little bit about the kind of literary achievement that it is, and then maybe say a little bit about the way in which one approaches the poem given that we'll be reading it in translation, and finally end with a little bit about Dante's life and times.

To begin, I think it's pretty clear to pretty much everyone that this is a remarkable, indeed unmatched, literary achievement in many ways. Dante takes as his subject nothing less than a journey to the three parts of the Christian afterlife, to hell, purgatory, and to heaven. Given that huge scope, pretty much anything is fair game in terms of subject matter for his readers to contemplate because he brings in such an enormous amount, both in terms of subject matter, and also in terms of dealing with the sorts of concerns that not only would be important to anybody alive on the planet in the 14th century, but also to anybody alive on the planet in our time as well.

Cook: Let me give you an example. A few years ago, Ron and I had the opportunity to teach Dante's *Divine Comedy* (or *Commedia*) in a maximum-security prison. We had just begun, and we were talking about one of the first sinners in hell, and an inmate put up his hand and said, "That's me, that's why I'm here. I did what she's doing right here in this poem." I think, in a way that for academics perhaps to hit us harder than ever before is the fact that this poem is really of universal significance and of contemporary value. Anyone who reads the poem seriously is going to confront himself or herself. Issues of our day as well as Dante's day because, although obviously we need some historical background, and we know that Dante's original audience is different than ourselves in many ways, nevertheless, the universality of Dante's concern, the extraordinary breadth of what he has to say, mean that this poem really can work on us, every bit as much as it worked on somebody living in Dante's time.

Herzman: Let me piggyback on what Bill said by giving another specific instance here. Like everybody else, Dante scholars were anxious to jump on the millennium craze, and they had a millennium conference, and all the advertisements went out and said this is your once in a thousand-year lifetime opportunity to sort of talk about Dante. They even had a slogan, and the slogan was, "When we get to the 21st century, we'll find that Dante is there waiting for us," and, corny as it sounded, I think it was not only effective but accurate because the sorts of concerns that are in the poem are the sorts of concerns that are of as much interest to people in the 21st century. So that, for example, it is a poem that deals with the way in which we have to wrestle with political institutions. How are we to be governed? What is justice and what is injustice? It deals with the idea of spiritual transformation. It deals with issues like what are good reasons for writing a poem and what are good reasons for reading a poem? So, the really big issues that folks have wrestled with turn out to be central to the *Commedia*, and what we want to try to do is try and give you the best possible entryway into those particular issues.

Cook: If you will, just as Virgil and later others are Dante's guide, the purpose of a guide is, of course, in a sense to make himself or herself irrelevant. That is our goal, too. If we're your guides through this particular reading of Inferno and Purgatorio and Paradiso, what we hope is you'll go back to the poem many times, and you'll find that, perhaps, memories of your guide are valuable, but you're now really ready to proceed on your own.

Herzman: So, to start, let's talk just a little bit about what makes the poem so complex. The first thing is, of course, it is very long. It's 14,000 lines long, and, as we said, divided into three parts, and each of those three parts is further subdivided. Dante invents a term, or, at least, gives new meaning to a term, "cantos," which simply means "songs," and they become the sort of chapter divisions of each of the three parts of the poem and, indeed, the poem as a whole. So there are 34 cantos in the Inferno, 33 in the Purgatorio, and 33 in the Paradiso, again, the grand total of 100. Each of those 100 cantos, itself a complex piece of work, and further subdivided according to another ingenious scheme that Dante develops, a particular way of rhyming things, a particular way of having a kind of small stanza that Dante calls *terza rima*, what would that be—third rhyme or triple rhyme.

Cook: Exactly, and so every canto has a number of these tercets, as we call them, this group of three lines, they average about 140 lines per canto. Nevertheless some are shorter, some are longer, but the rhyme scheme is extraordinarily important if you're going to understand the beauty of the language of the poem. To put it in its simplest terms, it's A B A, B C B. In other words, the first and third lines of one tercet rhyme with the second line of the next tercet, and then those first and third lines interlock with the middle line of the next tercet, and so on. So, it's an extraordinarily complex rhyme scheme—a lot easier to do, we might add, in Italian than it would be in other languages, for example—English would come to mind.

Herzman: What that means, of course, is that anybody dealing with it in a modern English translation is going to be faced with a very difficult problem—how do you handle the rhyme? Another way of looking at it, every word in Italian, or almost every word, ends in a vowel, which means that if you are rhyming, then what you can do is take any word and say, well, one word out of six is going to rhyme with it, all right? If you're doing that in English you have many more opportunities to have the rhyme, and therefore, rhyme itself is a much more difficult thing to accomplish. So the question is, what do you do if you are taking the poem from Italian and you are trying to put it into English? We want to say just a little bit about what some of the various modern translators have done in their attempt to deal with this issue, and the problem with translation in general, so that right from the beginning you can have a sense of how best to follow along in the poem yourself.

The first thing that I would say about the question of translation is this: If you were to take any five Dante scholars and put them in a room and say what is the best translation for somebody coming to the poem for the first time in English? You would get six different answers, okay, and the reason for that is not simply that Dante scholars are a cranky lot and don't want to agree with each other. It's that there are so many different variables that you have to play off, that what one considers important might not be what is considered most important by the next.

Again, let's take that question of rhyme. In our time, there has been one serious attempt to imitate Dante's *terza rima* in English, and while you can kind of admire it, I'm not sure that that's where you would want to go for your first time or even your second or even your third time through the poem, because, as it turns out, to get things to rhyme you have to do a little bit of forcing with the language, and it sounds very stilted, indeed, what it does is it sounds a bit forced. So, most of those who have decided to translate Dante into English will try to give some kind of sense of what the poetic line looks like. In other words, keep the three line stanzas, but not really rhyme, or at least not really continue the rhyme through the intricate pattern that Bill has established.

Cook: Not all, by the way, do that. There are prose translations of the *Divine Comedy*, and supposedly the advantage to them is because they don't have to worry at all about setting things up as a poem. They can be the most literal, and the most straightforward, and not have to worry about any of the artistry of the poem at all, and, although there is some value in reading the prose translation, perhaps for that reason, and I remember when a couple of my kids were in school, somehow or another poetry really put them off, but they would read a prose translation of Homer, for example, maybe there are some people for whom a purely prose translation is valuable. But certainly, most of the translations we have today, and the one we're going to use and the others we are going to talk about, are indeed ones that try to keep some sense of the poem as poem.

Herzman: Now, one of the exceptions to that turns out to be when people realize the limitations of prose, as Bill said, but also say look, what you've got is a poem in Italian, why not have Italian on one page, and then if you're going to use the other page, a prose translation might be good as long as you go over to the other side from time to time, and I think that this was intended, not only for people who have some grasp of Italian, but for people who have studied any of the related languages, so if you have done a little bit of Latin, a little bit of French, a little bit of Spanish, it would be possible to glance over at the Italian side and take a look at the English translation. In those cases, the prose might be a help, although, again, this is not the only way it is done. Simply to say that there are a ton of options out there to choose from.

Another problem with modern translation is that, as you can imagine, it is an enormous undertaking to translate a 14,000 line poem, and folks get started and publish their Inferno and say the other volumes are forthcoming, but they don't always come forth quite that quickly. So, there are a number of new translations that just came out, really terrific, but we don't know what the rest of it is going to be.

Just to give two examples in the last couple of years, both Robert Hollander and Robert Durling and his partner Martinez have come out with translations of the Inferno, but that's all we have, and, again, to our reckoning, these are both very good—facing page with dual language with neat notes, but, if you want to read the whole poem, they're not particularly valuable. Although, that does raise a very interesting question about do you need to take the whole thing from one translation, or can you read one Inferno, another Purgatory and another Paradise?

Cook: Obviously, there are arguments for both ways. If you read the same translation all the way through, you become very comfortable with the language, it flows as a poem, beginning in the dark wood of error and ending with Dante meeting God face to face. If you use different translations, obviously you have to readjust as you pick up each translation as each translator uses somewhat different principles, somewhat different degrees of literalness, or whatever. On the other hand, perhaps comprehensively after reading three different translations, you have a better sense of Dante as a whole, because each one can only draw some of the things that Dante does with his own original language of Italian.

Herzman: All that being said, what would we recommend in terms of a kind of relatively cheap, relatively accessible translation? For a long time John Ciardi's translations have been much used, and he has a poet's sensibility and his notes are okay, although not terrific. So that would be one option. Another, Alan Mandelbaum, is very nice because it's a cheap paperback edition. He's got on one side the Italian and on the other his own translation. The problem with Mandelbaum is his notes aren't all that great.

For English-speaking readers, the translation that is sort of standard is that of Charles Singleton, but the reason for that has a lot more to do with the fact that Singleton provides prodigious notes for the entire *Commedia*. So that, for example, what you get if you want to shell out the $130 or so that it cost for the Singleton edition three volumes of text and translation—three much, much thicker volumes of notes. While those notes are wonderful for the scholar, it might not be the most useful edition for the non-scholar. The notes can be a little bit overwhelming, maybe a little bit intimidating.

Cook: Sometimes those notes are of value only if you are studying Dante in the original Italian. In other words, it will talk about how Dante used this word variation rather than that word variation, and therefore those who are looking for the notes that help to provide the background to understand the poem find themselves skimming through some notes to find the ones that really get to the heart of what they want notes for. So, although, again, it's a great reference, it may not be the best thing to use your first time through for a reading where you want notes that give you the background that make the stories that Dante tells intelligible.

Herzman: All that being said, we can now sort of talk about the translation that we're going to use here and that we're going to be quoting from, Mark Musa's three-volume edition and translation of the *Divine Comedy*. Again, with all of what we've said, it serves clear we're not forcing this on you or saying that this is necessarily the best, but given the options it is the one we use with our undergraduates in class, and there are two good reasons for it.

One, I think he does a pretty good job with the translation itself, and also he sustains it throughout. My own impression is that as a translator he gets better as he gets rolling, and I think he does a very good job, for example, with the Paradiso, which I think is the hardest of the three canticles to translate. The other thing is Musa, it seems to us at any rate, has the best notes for somebody who is coming to the poem for the first time. It's to say, notes that are fairly comprehensive, will tell you most of what you need to know, but not intimidating and not overwhelming, and they don't assume that you've been reading the poem for a long time. Nothing particularly technical about what he does in the notes.

Cook: There's also a good introductory essay, and as in many translations, there are also things like diagrams of the various parts of the afterlife, and a very useful glossary at the back of each volume, so if you want to find a character, or a geographical place that Dante mentions, you don't have to skim back through all the notes, and it isn't really an index—it really is a glossary that's very, very handy in looking things up very quickly.

Herzman: Now, again, a lot of what we've said about edition leads to something else about the poem that gives it a kind of unique status. We've been talking about the notes, and I guess we need to say something about why one needs notes, why in most editions—certainly Musa's included—the notes are almost as long, and in some cases longer, than the text itself. This is sort of tricky business because it makes it seem as though the poem is totally inaccessible unless you're willing to do an awful lot of work outside of the poem. I think we probably should say at the outset that if somebody wanted to go through the poem, reading it and not looking at a single note, you would get an awful lot out of it. Dante does a number of things that make the poem accessible to the first-time reader, most of all because he is such a good story teller, that this journey that a pilgrim named Dante takes to the three parts of the after-world is an action-packed adventure story, and if you wanted to get it on no other level, you could do that, but most readers, and I think for good reasons, also see the necessity for notes, and that necessity was seen even in Dante's own time. In other words, you can get something, but there is more and the notes are an aid to that more.

Cook: The commentary tradition on the *Divine Comedy* began practically before the ink was dry on the 100th cantos. In fact, one of the first commentators on Dante's poem was one of his sons, and unlike almost any other of the world literature except the Bible, the tradition has been handed down now for almost 700 years of people doing line by line commentaries. You can find it on the Web; you can find it in many, many learned volumes, that every line has it's commentators so that one could do what scholars did in the Middle Ages for the Bible, and that is to say comment on every single verse. Obviously, again, these notes are a much watered-down version of this tradition. But, "Why do we need them at all?" I think is the question Ron raised. Let me suggest just one way of answering that question.

First, in general, when we read old books, the thing that strikes us is we're not the intended audience, and that, therefore, the original audience knew things that we just don't know, and in a sense, the commentary, the notes, the footnotes, are to sort of bring us up to snuff with Dante's original audience, or Homer's original audience, or Plato's original audience, or whatever. The reason that it is so much more complex for Dante than for almost any other of the great world authors is that in his journey through the afterlife, he just runs into so many folks and chats with them and they tell, sometimes straightforwardly, sometimes not, their own stories, and Dante expects his audience to have some general familiarity, if not with every character, at least the context out of which those characters came. That is to say, their political milieu, their social milieu, and whatever, and when almost all of the stories in the *Commedia* are Dante chatting with folks that he meets, not to know who many of those folks are after a while sort of becomes a burden to us, and there is a danger of sort of losing track of the story simply because here is another name I don't know followed by another name I don't know, and I can't tell whether this guy is telling his story straight or not because I never heard of this guy.

Herzman: Let me piggyback on that for a minute also. Bill has said that what you get is Dante encountering all of these interesting figures that he talks with in all three parts of the poem. While we need to know something about the figures in the three parts of the poem, we also need to know something about Dante himself, because the poet takes the very unusual and really daring move of making himself the "hero" of this poem. In other words, the person who encounters all of this is a guy named Dante, and helpful to access the poem is therefore something of an understanding of who Dante is and what his own life was about. In other words, the kind of biographical stuff surrounding Dante that we know as is present in the poem, and as is present in the commentary tradition about the poem, is not some kind of window dressing—it would be nice to know something about the author, I wish we knew about Homer in the way we know about Dante, I wish we knew more about Shakespeare—but, rather, what is going on here is that since he is the hero of his poem, and since he sets the poem "halfway" through his own life, we need to know as much as we can about that life, especially that first half, the first 35 years of it.

Cook: Let me give you an illustration. Dante, of course, is from the city of Florence. There are an awful lot of famous Florentines—Machiavelli, Michelangelo, and whatever—and if you go to Florence today and walk around the city you can visit, obviously, statues of Michelangelo in museums, you can visit Michelangelo's house, you can see the tomb of Machiavelli, but wherever you go in Florence you see Dante because what has happened is when Dante refers in his poem to a specific place in Florence, they'll tack up those lines in Italian on that building so that as you walk around Florence you realize how deeply rooted in this city, as well as in areas beyond the actual city limits, this poem is. You can't go two blocks in Dante's Florence, not quite as big as today's Florence, you can't go two blocks without finding a couple of lines here and a couple of lines there because the poem is so deeply rooted in his physical world—his own personal, political, social, cultural experiences—as a citizen of this late medieval city.

Herzman: So, let's talk just a little bit about Dante. He connects so importantly with the city of Florence, and that's a really good place to begin by saying simply that Dante was born in Florence in the year 1265, and that his family came from the merchant class of that city.

Cook: The city of Florence at that time probably had about 100,000 citizens. It was very, very tightly packed together, an area smaller than today's Florence, in fact, because you had to put up walls for medieval cities, and walls were expensive, therefore the smaller they are the less it costs to defend the place. So Dante was born in a hustling, bustling international mercantile-centered city. It doesn't look a lot today like it looked in Dante's day. The buildings that dominate the skyline today—the Cathedral of Florence and the City Hall—were, in fact, begun about the time that Dante left Florence for the last time. There certainly are some buildings that Dante was in— the building that he was baptized in, for example, the Baptistery of Florence, is in the earliest depictions of the city that we have. We don't even know how old that building is. So, Dante grew up in a merchant family in a time that was economically prosperous, the politically tumultuous, and as Dante the young man grew up, and we know almost nothing about his early years, it seemed that he developed two great passions. He was interested—passionately interested—and deeply involved in politics, and young Dante, it turns out, was also, surprise, surprise, a poet.

Herzman: So, that what we have is in his life (before he sets about writing the *Divine Comedy)* are records of what his political life was like. Fortunately, Dante was pretty successful as a politician and statesman as he grew up, but we also, of course, have records of his life as a poet. In particular, if you wanted to look at sort of the climax of this career, this "youthful" career as a poet, he wrote a work called the *Vita Nuova*, the New Life, which is a very interesting collection of love poems that he wrote to a woman named Beatrice, and put them together as a kind of a complete volume, a volume that somehow, through the poems, was meant to construct a kind of poetic autobiography, and in order to do that what he did was to take the poems, and then analyze them himself, giving a kind of commentary from his own life, and this work turns out to be an early masterpiece, which is of the magnitude that would be studied as an important work of Italian literature, of world literature, had Dante never written the *Commedia*. But, more important for our purposes is that this subject, other than Dante himself, of course, is this woman with whom he falls in love with, the woman named Beatrice, and the fact is that Beatrice becomes a very important character in the *Commedia*, indeed, becomes one of Dante's guides later on. So, as poet, he turns out to have had a very successful career before the *Commedia*, but the kind of stuff that he does, love poetry in particular, becomes important when we see the transition between the *Vita Nuova* to the *Commedia*.

Cook: Similarly, Dante had some real success politically. Florence didn't have what we would call a strong executive government, but rather every two months they changed officials, and there were six officials who served two-month terms, called "priors," and they were sort of the titular head committee of Florence for those two months. At the age of 35 in the year 1300, Dante became one of those priors for one of those two months, between June and August. He had really hit the big time, and even after those two months, he served important ambassadorial jobs as he had also before he served as prior. So Dante was a very successful political figure, but Florence was a deeply, deeply factionalized city. We'll talk more about the details of that in the next lecture, and ultimately the factionalism reached a head, and in 1301 when Dante was, in fact, away from Florence in Rome, his party, his faction, got kicked out, and Dante never returned to Florence. He was born there in 1265; he left for the last time in 1301. He lives the next 20 years of his life as an exile from his homeland.

Herzman: Notice that this is sort of interesting in terms of what we've already said about the year 1300, the year in which the poem is set. Dante takes the journey in 1300 at a time when in his real life he is at the height of his success, okay? A prior in the city of Florence, a successful poet, and yet he's writing the poem at a time when all of that success has gone down the tubes. He's writing the poem as an exile, and as an exile who really has no hope in returning to Florence. He spends the last 19 years of his life in that exile, and the fact is that he probably completes the poem only very shortly before his death. So, what we have is this paradox of the poem with Florence in some ways as its center, being written by somebody who is far away from Florence, wandering as in exile, and unable to come back to Florence.

Cook: Where did he go? Well, we know some parts of the answer to that question. For a while he stayed with his faction as they tried to overthrow the folks that had overthrown them. It seemed probably only in 1304 he gave that up. Then, we know he went to live in a variety of places, the most important of which was the city of Verona, in the north, your basic Romeo and Juliet town, and while in Verona it seems he did a good deal of the writing of the *Commedia*. Then, toward the end of his life he moved to the city of Ravenna, on the Adriatic coast. There he died. We actually have his death mask; it's in Florence. We can see what he looked like when he died, and there in Ravenna he is buried in a little chapel attached to the Franciscan church in Ravenna, and despite the fact the Florentines in modern times have wanted his body back and made a splendid tomb for him in Florence, he's in Ravenna.

Herzman: In fact, one of the ways that it's really kind of nifty to think about the poem is to think about the two tombs—the splendid one in Florence that doesn't have anybody in it, and the one in Ravenna, kind of grubby, out of the way, a nice sign over it that says tomb of Dante the poet, but the very lack of grandeur of that tomb is a very nice statement, I think, of this as a poem of exile that we'll be coming back to over and over again in our talk, the notion that it could not have been written except as a poem of exile. It has to be understood as a poem of exile.

So, as we move to the next lecture, we need to take up some of that political stuff that was responsible for his exile, and also begin to talk about how Dante makes this extraordinary poem.

Lecture Two
A Poet and His City—Dante's Florence

Scope:

Dante's poem puts heavy demands on its modern readers because Dante himself was so deeply involved in political issues that need to be retrieved from the past. This lecture will emphasize those political events in Dante's time that have the most direct impact on the poem. We will begin with a discussion of Florence, Dante's native city, and move to a discussion of Florentine society and politics, showing how the personal and the political were interrelated. This overview will give us the proper vantage point from which to view the struggle between Guelf and Ghibelline factions that was so prominent in Dante's time and is so important in the poem.

Outline

I. To be a member of Dante's afterlife, you must be dead by 1300.
   A. This includes people who died in 1299, Adam and Eve, and any number of those in between.
   B. Because so many of these figures were from Dante's lifetime or dealt with political issues that continued to be important in Dante's lifetime, commentaries have been written to bridge the gap between Dante and his readers.
   C. These commentaries are especially important to understand those figures who were part of the political scene that Dante surveyed.
   D. To describe this scene, we begin with the Florence of Dante's time.
      1. Florence in Dante's time was a tightly packed city of about 100,000 people.
      2. The population was socially diverse, with nobility, the middle class, and the poor living together in a very public existence where conversations were easily overheard.

II. Florentine politics was intensely local, and many sources of tension existed.

    A. Political strife was caused by disputes among local families. For instance, the breakup of an arranged marriage between two important households in 1215 led to a long-lasting blood feud.

    B. Political strife was also caused by different factions in the city as they jockeyed for power and quarreled over the best way to govern. The Verona of Shakespeare's *Romeo and Juliet*, with its rival clans trading insults and fighting in the streets, gives us an idea of what Dante's Florence must have been like.

III. Equally important, Florentine politics was also part of larger struggles taking place throughout Italy (then a region of many fiercely independent city-states) and Europe as a whole.

    A. Two major powers, the pope and the emperor, shaped the struggle as they contended for what amounted to world rulership.

    B. The Guelf faction supported the pope, while the Ghibellines supported the emperor.

    C. Emperor Frederick II Hohenstaufen, also king in southern Italy, tried to assert control over northern Italy starting around 1220.

IV. By 1300, the Guelfs had control over Florence, which was an economically important and strategically located city in the northern region known as Tuscany.

    A. The Ghibellines were a minority and relied heavily on external allies. In 1260, for instance, the Florentine Ghibellines joined with the rival city of Siena to defeat Florence at the Battle of Monteperti.

    B. Internal struggles developed among the Guelfs, and in 1300, the party split into two factions, the Whites and the Blacks.

    C. Both sides appealed for papal support, although the struggle was more over power than any religious or ideological principle.

        1. Pope Boniface VIII supported the Black Guelfs and sent his troops to expel the Whites, which was the direct cause of Dante's exile.

    2. Boniface—though still alive in 1300—is a major character in the *Commedia.*

V. Dante's exile is a necessary condition for the writing of the poem.

    A. The issues of exile themselves become part of the poem.

    B. Exile, for Dante, can be spiritual and eternal, as well as physical and transitory.

    C. During exile, Dante studied, meditated, and learned much of what makes the *Comedy* such an impressive poem.

    D. The poem can be seen as Dante's way of making sense of his exile—indeed, it is a song of exile, permeated by that theme at every level.

        1. Dante began by trying to figure out how to escape his exile.

        2. He then turned to deep and broad study and thought to learn how to come to grips with his exile and make something good come of it.

    E. Dante believed that this life is not the ultimate end, but that it is important both in itself and because it is where one's eternal destiny is shaped.

Readings:

Daniel L. Bornstein, trans., *Dino Compagni's Chronicle of Florence,* Books 1–2.

Joan Ferrante, *The Political Vision of the Divine Comedy,* Introduction, Chapters 1–3.

Questions to Consider:

1. Why is Dante's biography so vital in understanding the *Commedia*? Can the political situation in Florence in Dante's time fully explain what Dante is trying to do?

2. Given that the pope and the emperor were both headquartered far from Florence, why did it matter so much to them who controlled the city?

Lecture Two—Transcript
A Poet and His City—Dante's Florence

Cook: As we said in the last lecture, much of the *Commedia* involves Dante traveling to the afterlife, meeting up with a whole bunch of folks, many of whom most of us, even those who are scholars, really don't know from their study of the past. Therefore, what we want to do today is to begin to help with the understanding of the peopling of Dante's afterlife. We want to set up the rules of the game, to a great extent, and then begin to talk especially about the political background because—especially in Inferno, but really throughout the entire poem—Dante is going to be making political commentary through not only his own mouth and the mouth of Virgil and his other guides, but also through the mouths of so many of these folks whom he runs into.

Herzman: One way of getting at this issue is to go to a question that I usually ask my students when we begin looking at Dante. The question is simply this: What do you need to get your membership card in Dante's afterlife? I usually ask the question and somebody puts up a hand and says, "You need to be dead." I say, "That's the right answer, what's the second part?" Usually somebody else says, "You need to be dead by 1300," which is, of course, as we said in the last lecture, the actual date of the journey from the point of view of the pilgrim.

It's interesting if you think about this. First of all, it allows Dante the poet to have an enormous scope here in terms of who the pilgrim is going to encounter, because what it means is that this includes folks that died in 1299, it also includes Adam and Eve, actually Adam and Eve will show up as characters in the Paradiso, it also includes everybody in between. Notice that means everybody. Dante does not distinguish between what we would think of as real people— historical characters who actually lived, and folks who come from books—characters in books. So, for example, we get to see Aeneas. He's a character even though he was a creation of Virgil, who also turns out to be a character there—so, dead by 1300, real or fictional.

The thing is, a lot of those folks are very famous, and a lot of those folks are famous in our time as well as in Dante's time. You've got people from the Bible who played a prominent role and all kinds of political figures who have made a very big impact on world history, and all of those folks turn out to be people that we know something about but maybe would like to know a little bit more. So, commentaries are certainly necessary for them, but even more important, what we need to do is talk about the figures who are dead by 1300 who are folks who lived in Dante's Florence or in any of the neighboring cities and whose fame, really, was a kind of local fame. In other words, folks who would have been pretty well known in Dante's time and place, but not well known at all, maybe not even known at all, in our own time. So, a good bit of what we are going to be doing now is to try and bridge that gap by talking about the scene that Dante grew up in.

Cook: Let's remember also that if Dante wants to talk about politics and other facets of Florentine life, an Italian life around 1300, he—by and large—cannot use his own contemporaries directly to do that because Dante is 35 years old in 1300, and therefore most of his colleagues and friends and contemporaries, his political buddies and his political enemies, are still alive. That, to look at contemporary politics, Dante will sometimes, indeed, go way back into ancient history, we'll meet Alexander the Great and Julius Caesar and the Emperor Trajan, for example. But, more often he tends to go back, if you will, one generation—the generation of his parents and perhaps his grandparents—and there's a good reason for that. One is that most of them are dead and therefore they fit the rule, but the second thing is that these are the stories that Dante himself grew up with.

Now, Ron and I were both born in the same year. We were born toward the end of World War II, so we don't remember World War II or another event in our parents' lives, the Depression, but boy did we grow up hearing the stories about it. There are times when you sort of have to remember, you know, I only know this stuff because of other people telling me the stories. I really wasn't around during the Depression, I wasn't really around and functioning during World War II, and that's what Dante is going to do. We're going to have an awful lot of folks populate Dante's afterlife that have died pretty recently because not only are they people who are still remembered by Dante's audience, but he can use them and the stories he knows about them not only to talk about a little bit of recent history, but in many ways, symbolically at any rate, to talk about the present—to talk about what is going on right here, right now. A different cast of characters (sometimes different labels on the political factions), the basic problems have not changed very much since the generation before Dante and his contemporaries.

Herzman: So, we're going to start with that generation and, even though Dante himself will not limit himself to talking about Florence, Florence certainly is the center and certainly is the focus. So, before we talk about some people we'll talk about where they lived, what kind of a place was Florence in the generation before Dante?

Cook: As we said in the last lecture, it was a busy, bustling, high-population, high-density city surrounded by walls, and that means life is lived largely outdoors. It means that people knew each other's faces; they knew each other's business; they knew lots of personal things about them. After all, housing didn't have lights and heat and a lot of other things, and even today, when one is in Italy, one finds that there are times of day when people just go out and stroll to be seen. So, it was a life lived much more publicly, much less privately, and therefore, if we're going to talk about the politics of Dante's Florence, that is where we have to start. That is to say, if you ask the question who doesn't like whom, there are a lot of ways to approach that. We can approach it, for example, as socially. That is to say, those who were parts of the old, rural aristocracy and had moved, don't like the *nuevo riche*, and that's a very important problem in Florence, for example. But, a lot of times, the people you don't like, and this takes on political ramifications in Florence, are your neighbors, somebody who insulted you, somebody who insulted your sister, somebody who threw garbage around your house, and we know that a lot of the quarrels began with very personal things, and there's a very personal side to Florentine politics. The story that both Dante and contemporary chroniclers tell of the beginning of factionalism in Florence goes back to a guy who snubbed a woman he was supposed to marry when he got a better offer. That, perhaps, is literally true, it happened in 1215, but much more important it is symbolically true, and we never want to forget the sort of visceral, gut, local side of Florentine politics, and that will come out over and over and over when Dante meets Florentines again largely of the previous generation.

Herzman: We remind ourselves of that 1215 story; first of all it turns out Dante uses it in the *Commedia* itself, but we think about it. Okay, a person was snubbed, and so, let's not talk to them for a while. I was going to marry her, but they gave me a better offer. I'll marry the other one instead. Well, that's not how it ended. It ended with a lot of people, starting with the bridegroom, being killed, and an awful lot of straight-out, hard-core violence was the result of this, and that violence kind of continued. If you look at 1215 as a starting point, it certainly had not diminished by the time that Dante sets the poem, and it certainly hadn't diminished in that generation immediately before the setting of the poem. So, we're talking about the existence of a lot of urban violence. People died in the streets. The stuff that you read about in *Romeo and Juliet* is sort of based on what was actually happening in the factionalistic struggles that were taking place in the cities of Italy.

Cook: Ron's exactly right. We need to think about a lot of violence, not always leading to death, but insults and all the rest that really did inflame people, and one of the reasons it got so testy and violent is because, needless to say, people, both those of the traditional aristocracy and the *nuevo riche* wanted power. That's what you want—political power. Being able to control the legal mechanisms, the judiciary and other parts of the city as well, and there are only so many offices to go around. So, at least as one chronicler contemporary with Dante describes it was a competition for offices, it made things so violent, so visceral, so constantly factional, that there were always these fights because if these folks held office then these folks didn't, and if these folks held office they can use that for their advantage to install themselves, ideally, in perpetuity in office. So, there is a great deal of competition for power. Only so many titles, only so many jobs to go around.

But this is only the beginning of understanding Florentine politics. As I said, there are also social distinctions; there are economic distinctions that don't always fit the social categories. You get, again, some very wealthy merchants who don't come from very important families, and, of course, they have money that they can use to gain power over the traditional nobility, and these kinds of tensions are also very clear. We'll see people from that aristocracy, for example, snub Dante even when Dante's looking in on them, oh let's say, somewhere in the middle of hell. They'll still sort of say, "You're not from a very important family; you're not from a family that can be traced back as many generations as my family can be traced back." It's more complicated than that because in addition to what's going on inside the walls of Florence, Florence exists in a bigger world.

For one thing, of course, Florence was an independent nation. Italy as a country only came along in the 19th century, and so Florence's independent neighbors, for example, are Arezzo and Siena and Pisa and Luca, and so forth, and these are independent countries too, and guess what? Independent countries fight, and they fight over many of the things that we would expect. They fight over whether that castle that is sort of on the border is yours or mine. If we get this little piece, we have access to some more water that would flow into an area of our nation, and so on. So, there is a great deal of regional fighting over exactly the kinds of things you would expect—over border lines, over water rights, over access to highways, and all that sort of stuff.

Herzman: Notice that we started locally. We've moved out a little bit to the neighboring city-states. We can move out even more and talk about causes for factionalism and political dispute in the larger circumstances of European politics as a whole, because even as there were all of these independent city-states in the part of Italy that Dante is from, there were also larger—I'm not sure world powers would be the best way of describing them—but at least larger European powers that also exhibited a lot of clout. Not simply, let's say, in the case of the Holy Roman Emperor, one of those two powers, not simply in the territory where he had residence, but throughout Europe. The other sort of political clout that was exercised in Europe as a whole and in Italy as a whole was with the pope. So, to start locally and move out, we now need to be a little bit more global in talking about the place of emperor and pope in the European political scene, and then sort of take it back locally and see how it affects Florence.

Cook: So, Florence is a little nation in the whole European scheme, but a very important one because of its economic power and because of its geographical location. Well, there were, in the early Middle Ages, of course, the development of the papacy, the office of the Bishop of Rome, although it was much more a tradition than a government in the early Middle Ages, and there was a development of the Holy Roman Empire, beginning with Charlemagne in 800, rejuvenated by Otto the Great in the 10th century, but—by and large—those officials and those powers were not in direct conflict. Beginning toward the end of the 11th century they were in big-time conflict, and the ultimate question was: Who rules the world?

It's a pretty big question. That is to say, ultimately, when push comes to shove, obviously it is best if they work together, who really is first and foremost in charge? Who has the authority from God to rule in the world? In the 13th century, the century into which Dante is born, that question took a particular political form that involves us thinking for a minute of a map of Italy. If you divide Italy as you go down the boot into three sections, it will help. The top third, roughly, is a series of independent nations of which Florence is one of the most important. The middle third, roughly, was controlled by the pope—not just as a spiritual center, but as political territory. They had all the rights over the center part of Italy that any secular ruler had. The southern third was governed by a monarchy. It was a monarchy, for a while, of French, but it was a strong monarchy that included everything from, say, a little bit north of Naples, including the island of Sicily. So this is the political scheme.

What happens around 1220 is this: The guy who is the monarch of southern Italy and Sicily, also gets elected Holy Roman Emperor, and in theory, the Holy Roman Emperor is sort of the lord over these northern Italian city-states. Not much in practice, but in theory. But this emperor and king, Frederick II, Frederick Hohenstaufen is his name, has an idea. I'd like to really get control of those northern Italian city-states. I'd like that to be not just in spirit, but in fact my territory, and I'm already king of the south. Okay, you can picture what this does. It means the pope has the same neighbor on the north and on the south, and as it turns out, Frederick was not a friendly neighbor, and a knock-down-drag-out struggle began between the papacy and the Holy Roman Empire for control of Italy, and in some real way control to be *numero uno* in Europe at this time.

Herzman: A couple of comments to make about that: First of all, keep this in mind because Frederick himself becomes a player in the *Commedia*; he is someone we will see later on, but notice what this does to the story that we started out with, the story in Florence. You now have two competing world powers, two competing ideologies, and you have these smaller city-states, Florence, for our purposes, chief among them. When the factionalism in Florence develops, one side fighting against another, there is kind of a natural tendency to go to the big guys on the outside to seek support. Well, the folks who wanted to seek this support from the emperor were called "Ghibellines," and the folks who wanted to seek this support from the pope were called "Guelfs," and all of a sudden, in Florence and in all of the city-states surrounding Florence, the struggles that were going on sort of the umbrella term—the struggle between Guelfs and Ghibellines—become a way of capturing something of what was going on, showing the linkage between what was going on in the city and what was going on in the larger theatre of European and world politics.

Cook: So, let's get specific for a second. Let's say you are part of a faction in Florence that's in the minority. What you will do, then, perhaps, is go to one of those super powers and say, "Hey, we'll be your guise in this territory." They really aren't interested in the ideology of the pope's so much, or the ideology of the emperor, what they want is help. What they want to do is take over their own place. They want to be in charge, and since in Florence, the Ghibellines were traditionally the minority, they depended very heavily on sort of outsiders helping them out militarily and politically to try to get control of this place. The time we're going to focus on is a time in 1260, let me tell you how far this can go, where the Ghibellines of Florence allied with the city of Siena, it's southern neighbor which was dominated by Ghibellines, and together they fought the army of Florence, which at that time was dominated by Guelfs, at a very famous battle named the Battle of Montaperti in 1260. The Ghibellines won, and therefore the Ghibellines took over Florence even though Florence had more Guelfs than Ghibellines. They took over temporarily. It was during that six-year rule of the Ghibellines that a fellow named Dante was born in Florence in 1265, and when Dante is one year old, the Ghibellines are kicked out and his party, the Guelfs, came back into power. You see what I mean? These are the stories that Dante grows up with. These are the stories of the control over Florence. It is not about Papal and imperial ideology primarily, although the propaganda is used to fuel the hostilities. It is about—to a much greater extent—local control, local power, local seizing, and control over offices.

Herzman: Now, you would think Ghibellines are out, Guelfs take over, well, jeepers, maybe some of this factionalism will stop. It turns out that the Ghibellines never came back into Florence as a powerful force. So, you have Florence as a Guelf city and it remains a Guelf city, and it remains a happy, contented city—well, not hardly.

Cook: Not quite, because, well, this has happened before and it has happened since in politics. If basically one party comes to dominate guess what happens? Squabbles break out within the party over the same old issues: insults, social standing, and all the rest, and so in the 1290s, Dante's an adult by this time, in the 1290s we begin to get real new factions developing, not between Guelfs and Ghibellines— Ghibellines are minor players by now, at least in Florence, we get divisions within the Guelf party, and it gets very bitter in the way that former friends who become enemies become very bitter.

We call these two factions of the Guelfs the "Whites" and the "Blacks," simply by colors that sort of identified them, sort of armbands if you will. So, Dante gets caught up in factional politics, the next generation, and the next generation is within the Guelfs rather than between the Guelfs and the Ghibellines, and so, since the Holy Roman Emperor at this time is pretty weak in terms of Italy, each faction goes to the strongest political power in Italy and says, "You back us." The strongest political faction in Italy is the papacy, and by 1294, the papacy was headed by a fellow, again, we'll hear a lot about him in Dante, named Pope Boniface VIII.

Herzman: What happens, of course, is that they're both looking for the support from Boniface, the Whites and the Blacks, but Boniface is only going to give his support to one, and as it turns out, for a variety of reasons, Boniface supports the Black Guelfs rather than the White. He sends his troops to expel the Whites, and it turns out that that is the direct cause of Dante's own exile. The circumstances are kind of interesting, and it's worth us saying a little bit more about it because Boniface, too, is really a major player, a really important character, in Inferno and mentioned throughout the whole *Commedia.* So, a little bit more here might seem to be, you know, a little bit more detail than you would want at this point. Trust us, it's going to be important as it goes on. A little bit more about Boniface and his relationship to the struggles in Florence is necessary.

Cook: It's first of all important to say that Boniface himself was a native of a town near Rome. He actually was a native of the Papal states, and becoming the pope meant that he was involved in the governance of central Italy, the Papal states, and guess what? There are factions there too. Different families and his family had been in and out of power as popes in the 13th century, and they had terrible and vicious enemies among other families with church offices in the

Papal states. So, he's involved in a knock-down-drag-out struggle for political control over the area that he's supposed to be able to govern.

At the same time, he's also in a knock-down-drag-out economic and political struggle with the French king, because basically what the French king wants is more money from the church and more control of the Church by his own office, and therefore taking away some power from the pope. So, Boniface is involved in two major political struggles—one in central Italy, and one we would say international. What's important to see is, Boniface, who himself was a canon lawyer by trade and very old when he became pope, was almost totally consumed during his nine-year pontificate in these two separate, although occasionally they overlapped, these two separate political campaigns—one largely of paper and propaganda, the other sometimes of swords and spears.

Herzman: Now, we mentioned that all of this is going to be necessary for us because the cast of characters, Boniface himself, Frederick the Holy Roman Emperor, a great many other people who were directly and indirectly involved in first the Guelf/Ghibelline struggle and then the White/Black struggle are going to be seen in the *Commedia*, but, of course, in fact, the most important person that this struggle affects is Dante himself because once the pope backs the Black Guelfs, then Dante, a White Guelf, is doomed. That is to say, Boniface's decision to support the Black Guelfs and send his troops to expel the Whites was the direct cause of Dante's own exile, and, as we mentioned at the beginning, Dante's exile is one of the most important things that we need to consider as a kind of condition for writing the poem, but also the issues of his exile, the issues of this whole struggle—this issue on a local level, and this issue on a national level, and this issue on an international level. All of this becomes a subject of the poem itself.

Cook: We need, therefore, to sort of stop for a second and say, sort of flat out, that this is a poem of exile. It is unimaginable that Dante would have written something sort of just a little bit different had he remained sort of fat and comfortable in Florence for the rest of his life. It is permeated with the theme of exile, from Dante's statement at the very beginning about being lost in a dark wood of error, through various characters he meets who, in fact, tell us of various ways they dealt with political rejection and exile, to some of the great theological issues he raises that are perhaps challenging to him because of his situation as an exile. At every level of reading this poem, it is a work of exile.

Herzman: There are a couple of ways to think about this to add to what Bill has said. First of all, it's highly unlikely that the poem would ever be written without the exile simply because it provides subject matter, okay, but there is another way to look at it as well because it seems that what happens is that in the early years of Dante's exile, what he was mostly concerned with was thinking of ways in which he could possible get back, okay, sort of making alliances and assuming that this was just a kind of temporary situation since there always had been this fluctuation that, okay, the Blacks are in power now, but if we hang around for a while we'll be able to get back. That didn't happen, all right? It seems like that at a certain point in the exile Dante really turned his attention elsewhere. That is to say, instead of trying to figure out the best way of getting back from exile, he began to think about the larger meaning of exile and to do this it was not just sort of simply pondering the state of the universe in a vacuum. Dante, or so it seems, set about systematically to read and study and meditate and make himself essentially one of the most learned people ever to put pen to ink, or quill to ink I guess in his case.

Cook: We, therefore, need to see that what Dante is doing here is trying to come to grips on enormously different levels of reality with exile. Obviously, there is a way in which you come to it theologically. We are all, in a sense, exiles from the promised land of heaven. It becomes a metaphor for the human condition generally. But also, Dante sort of racks his brain to say, "What is so unjust about the way we're governing ourselves, and what might we do about this? How can we untangle this maze to try to understand the way we could live together well?" Because Dante understood that the goal of human life was not earthly happiness, but that earthly happiness a) was important, and b) was a pretty good condition for people being able to seek those things that do last beyond the grave. If you're simply grubbing around to survive, and you know that the way to survive is to stab, literally or metaphorically, somebody else in the back, you're probably not going to be focused on those things that last forever.

Herzman: So, when he's reading and studying in his exile, obviously he reads a lot of works that are classic works on politics, but also he goes to others who have either suffered from—or written about—exile themselves, and it turns out to be a pretty long list of poets, and it also turns out to be the case that he can go to sources like the Bible, and Bill started off by saying that exile really is ultimately a kind of spiritual condition, and has to do with all of us who are separated from our home. That's the sort of stuff that Dante began to think about in a way that few others have, and so that when he begins to write the poem he has not only the experience of exile, the meditation on it in his personal life, but also a huge number of texts at his disposal, which deal with that central issue. When we start talking in the next lecture, we'll begin looking at those texts that Dante himself drew upon in his own *Commedia*.

Lecture Three
Literary Antecedents, I

Scope:

This lecture explains how Dante makes use of earlier literature in his poem. Dante's three guides in the *Commedia* show how his journey is a combination of the universal and the particular. In writing about this journey, the poet goes to many literary sources as a way of tapping the energy of existing traditions and putting them in dialogue with his own concerns, thus universalizing his poem without losing a sense of its particularity. In this lecture, we will emphasize the most important of these other texts, starting with the Bible. We will discuss how the Bible was read in the Middle Ages and show some of the ways that the *Commedia* can be seen as an imitation of the Bible. We will also talk about the importance of Virgil's *Aeneid* as a source for Dante.

Outline

I. Dante draws energetically and systematically on other texts in the *Commedia*.

    A. He builds on what previously exists.

    B. His rewriting of other texts provides him with a source of energy and with some of the organizational principles for his poem.

    C. He brings together the biblical and the classical traditions in his use of these texts.

    D. For Dante, the Bible does not obscure the value of non-Judeo-Christian texts, but instead provides lenses through which to read them.

II. The Bible is, not surprisingly, Dante's most important source.

    A. The Bible was seen as a record of God's working in history, from creation to last judgment. It tells a story with a beginning and an end.

    B. The Bible was seen as "God's other book," providing a key to and commentary on the universe itself, the first "book" authored by God.

C. Medieval folk saw the Bible more as a unity than do modern scholars, who tend to analyze it into its various parts and sources.

III. We must understand the Bible as it was read in the Middle Ages, that is, typologically.

    A. The Old Testament was seen in its relationship to the New Testament.

        1. Events in the Old Testament were considered historical and important in their own right, but neither complete nor completely binding (e.g., Mosaic dietary and ritual laws).

        2. Figures in the Old Testament looked forward to Christ.

            a. David is one such example; he is an ancestor of Jesus and prefigures the roles of Jesus as priest, prophet, and king.

            b. The prophet Jonah is another example; his exit from the whale's belly prefigures the Resurrection.

            c. John says that the "manna from heaven" in the Old Testament prefigures the "bread of life" in the New.

    B. This perspective allows people to make use of stories that are in some ways distant in time and place, as the stories of Hebrew Scripture would be to people living in the Middle Ages. For a modern example, consider what the Exodus story meant to American blacks under slavery and segregation.

IV. Dante makes use of this way of looking at the Bible in his own poem. Events in the *Commedia* are typologically related to other parts of the poem, especially in terms of the relationship between the three canticles.

V. Dante also makes use of the biblical prophets, incorporating the spirit of prophecy into the *Commedia.*

    A. Prophets do not mostly or merely foretell the future; they are rooted in the past and "forth-tell" divinely inspired but hard-to-hear truths out of an intense concern with the present.

    B. Dante wants to imitate this "forth-telling": He is a prophetic voice concerning his own times.

VI. Dante's guide for two-thirds of the poem is the Roman poet Virgil (70–19 B.C.E.).

    A. Virgil lived during the reign of Augustus, the first Roman emperor. He leaves the scene only at the end of the Purgatorio.

    B. His great epic poem the *Aeneid* was a model and a source for—and sometimes a rival to—Dante's *Commedia*.

        1. The *Aeneid* tells the story of how Aeneas, a Trojan prince, abandoned his burning city and went west to found Rome.

        2. Dante makes typological use of the *Aeneid*, pervasively echoing—and rewriting—it in the *Commedia*.

Readings:

Bible, Genesis 1–3, Exodus 1–19.

A. C. Charity, *Events and Their Afterlife*, Chapters 1–2.

Peter Hawkins, *Dante's Testaments*, Part I.

Questions to Consider:

1. Dante says in Inferno 2 that he is not Aeneas. Although that is obviously true on a literal level, is there a way in which Dante in fact becomes Aeneas?

2. Dante might have chosen a Christian or a great philosopher, such as Aristotle, as his guide. Why does he choose Virgil?

Lecture Three—Transcript
Literary Antecedents, I

Herzman: At the end of the last lecture we talked a little bit about Dante as a learned poet, somebody who meditated on and appropriated to himself a number of very, very important texts that really were part of earlier traditions. What we want to do in a somewhat more systematic way today is talk about the way, in fact, that Dante was able to use those texts in the *Commedia* itself, the way in which he was able to build on what previously existed so that he would be able to deal with issues that are at a pretty sophisticated level, taking what was already there as a kind of starting point. So, what we are going to do is suggest that these other texts really become for him a source of energy and also help to account for some of the organizational principles of his own poem. To do that, we're going to start with the blockbuster of all texts, the text that was most fundamental to the way Dante thought and wrote, and that text, of course, would be the Christian Bible.

Cook: First of all, it is hard, I think, even today for Christians to understand how central the Bible was to people in the Middle Ages, because it was not just the source of their religious ideas, of their organization of their churches, and whatever, but it was a mind in which one could find valuable stuff about every conceivable subject, obviously things related to purely religious and theological things such as ethics, but also politics, raising your child, or whatever it might be, the Bible was seen as a source of a different kind than all other sources. It didn't block out the value of non-biblical, non-Judeo-Christian texts, but everything in some ways was seen through the prism of the Bible's standards, and therefore we need to start with this extraordinary thing. Of course, one of the difficulties in talking about the Bible is it isn't a book. That is to say, it is a collection, an anthology, of Hebrew literature and the earliest Christian literature, and today a lot of modern scholarship emphasizes the different origins of books or parts of the books and recreates the historical context in which Isaiah wrote or the evangelist John wrote or whatever it might be, and that's all well and good. Dante would not have known a lot of that stuff, or probably cared very much about that sort of stuff that we call a lot of biblical scholarship today. Rather, the Bible was a book of life; it was a story. It was a story that had a beginning and a story that had an end.

It had huge narrative pieces, but also beautiful poetry. It was a literary model as well as a book of information and a guide, and I think we need to have that comprehensive understanding of the Bible before we can see what it is that Dante is going to do with those texts.

Herzman: I want to add to what Bill said in terms of the importance of the Bible again by suggesting some differences between the way it is looked on now and the way it was looked at back then. It's important to see this not simply as a book or even a collection of books, although it was that, but that those books themselves were seen to be a record of acts—that is to say, the action of God working in history. As Bill suggested it had a plot, okay, and that plot, to be a little bit more specific, goes from creation all the way to Last Judgment, and so somebody looking at that book would see all of human history contained in it, and therefore see one's self implicated in that story. In other words, you look at the Bible and you say, "Yes, that tells us about how God acted in history, but it's also telling us about how he acts in history, and as such, part of what we have to do is learn how to read it appropriately so that we can learn how to see the meaning in history, the meaning of our own lives, the meaning of our own actions." Okay? So, it's important, again, to kind of try to develop this medieval mindset when we think about the way in which Dante mined the Bible.

Cook: In other words, I think what Ron's suggesting, if I can sort of build on his thought, is that today it's easy to look at the Bible as a historical record of a people who lived a long time ago, that the last dot was put on the last sentence of the Bible 1,900+ years ago, perhaps, and therefore it seems very different from the world we inhabit. It seems like a strange place, if you will, this biblical world just as ancient history seems like a strange place, and obviously today one of the things the sermons do, for example, is try to bridge that gap. In many ways, in the Middle Ages, it was a much more systematic enterprise. First of all they didn't believe there was nearly as big a gap to bridge. Secondly, there was this constant dialogue, conscious dialogue, between the past and the present. Not what did the Bible mean for those folks, what does it mean for me? Not just in terms of general ideas or an occasional favorite story to draw a moral from, but as Dante later on himself line by line by line—what did this mean then, what does this mean now, what will this mean for our future, which also, again, is going somewhere toward an end that is described prophetically at the end of the Bible in the Book of Revelation.

Herzman: Another way that they looked at the Bible, they were pretty clear about the fact that God wrote it. They were not literalists, or fundamentalists perhaps would be a better term, as we sometimes suspect they were, but the fact is they were convinced that these Scriptures were sacred. They were authored by God, and this showed God's workings in history in the same way that "God's other book" did, which was the universe itself. In other words, that sense of creation, since we are created and since there is a creator, one of the very best images they had to sort of think about that process was that creation was like a "book" authored by God, and that sort of set the relationship right for them. Well, if creation was, if you will, God's first book, the Bible turned out to be not only his second and parallel book, but as many figures in the Middle Ages put it, it was the interpretive key to his first book. In other words, one reads the Bible in order to discover things about the first book authored by God about the universe itself. So, again, this sense of the Bible as a source, we need to start with all of these things that give it a place that, as Bill put it at the very beginning of this lecture, very difficult for us to kind of relate to because of modern ways that we have of looking at this text.

Cook: Let me illustrate this beginning with a story that everybody is familiar with, the story of creation in Genesis. I think this is a way that medieval people would look at this story. First of all it says that humans are created in the image of God. Therefore, the more you know about God, the more you know about humans. After all, it doesn't make much sense to say I understand the image of God without understanding what it is that is being imaged.

The second thing is, in that same creation story in Genesis, God gives certain commands to humans, and he gives them certain things that other people don't have, or other creatures don't have. So, people could talk, for example. Well, other creatures can't. So God endows them with certain gifts, and then says go out and use those gifts in imitation of me. Be fruitful and multiply. Fill the earth and subdue it, rule over, and so on and so forth. So, if you will, what humans are, and what humans image, is all laid out at the beginning, and every word of the Bible quite literally was seen therefore to be a guide to knowing God, and therefore also a guide to knowing human conduct.

Herzman: Okay, so we have established the importance of the text. What we need to talk about next is how they went about reading it. Given its importance, they spent a lot of time saying, "Well, there are good ways to read it and not so good. What are the best ways?" They were very concerned about the fact that the Bible, you open it, and it's divided into two parts. The Old Testament, which is the story of a people, chosen by God as the story goes, the Hebrews, and that story is given right from the time of Abraham all the way through the ups and downs of their history, but if you want the continuation of that story in the New Testament, then it kind of changes focus a little bit and talks about the impact of one particular Hebrew, Jesus Christ. So, you have this stark division, really, between the Old and the New Testament.

One of the issues they had to deal with in a very explicit way was what was the relationship between these two different bodies of literature? Written at different times, written in different languages— the Old Testament was originally written in Hebrew, the New Testament originally written in Greek, and, in fact, seeming to deal with different things. Is there a way to make sure that we see some kind of continuity, some kind of connection, between these two parts of the Bible?

Cook: Another way to put it is something like this: That you've got the Old Testament with all of the stories and laws and rules and regulations. Clearly it is sacred Scripture for Christians, and clearly Christians are to be guided by it. On the other hand, there are many specific parts of the Old Testament that Christians regard as not binding. For example, Christians don't practice the dietary regulations of Jews, nor are they circumcised, at least by religious ritual, and so how do you deal with this body of literature that a) is sacred, is the writing of God, and b) is problematic given the way Christians live, and even given some of the things that New Testament writers say.

Herzman: Well, one of the ways they look at it is by saying what's the most central thing that happens in this story that begins with creation and that ends with the Last Judgment at the end of time? To Christians, it was God entering the world in the form of Jesus Christ, God's son. Well, what they did was say how are we going to take

©2001 The Teaching Company

that and look at the previous history of the Hebrews, and how are we going to see that previous history in relation to this event? What they did was say there is a relationship, and the relationship is as follows: Those events that took place in the Old Testament; they are, for the most part, historically true. They are important to know and understand in and of themselves, but they are not complete in themselves because we don't really know what the story means, what the full story means, until we see how they are related to those events that connect with the life of Christ in the New Testament. In other words, what they did was develop in a fairly systematic way a relationship between people and events in the Old Testament, and the person and the events in the life of Christ in the New Testament, and systematically studying and exploring that relationship turns out to be a large part of what occupied the mind of, what we would call, biblical scholars, of people who wrote and commented about the Bible in the Middle Ages.

Cook: That word systematic that Ron used is really clear because in the New Testament itself, there are suggestions of this. Paul talks about all the prophets really talking about Jesus. John talks about that the real "bread of life" is not the manna in the desert but is Jesus coming down from heaven. What happens in the centuries just before, and in Dante's own century, is the attempt to make this systematic, line-by-line, correspondent-by-correspondent. You'll see, for example, in which you'll have a whole strip of Old Testament stories, and then right next to them, usually with some sort of visual connection, you will see their New Testament analogs, or New Testament fulfillment. So, it does become quite a system, and Dante—we don't know quite how his education all unfolded—really was deeply initiated into not just the idea of doing this, but the system and the thoroughness of doing it line-by-line, story-by-story.

Herzman: So, again, to use a couple of specific examples from biblical acts of Jesus that will set us up to see the way that Dante does it, what they did was take a look at a very important figure, let's say, in Hebrew Scripture, like King David, say that if you look at David in the various roles that he plays, as king, as shepherd, as somebody who is very important in the development of the Hebrew's sense of their own identity, those same attributes were given to Jesus who was seen to be a king in the line of David. So, if you look at what you have with the story of David, from this perspective, everything you see about him in Hebrew Scripture is real and important, but it's not the whole story. You have to know how the story comes out before you can see the way that works.

Cook: One illustration that is often given to sort of begin our discussion of this is to say that we've got the story of Jonah and the whale, the famous story from the book of the prophet Jonah, and the whale, or the fish, swallowed Jonah and three days later he's spit up on the shore. Well, there's a clue even in the New Testament that says this is linked to Jesus. Just as Jonah was in the belly of the whale and came out, so was Jesus in the belly of the earth, in the grave, and then he came out on the third day as well. So, that's the kind of way that we find these very specific connections all the way through. You'll find pictures in the Middle Ages, again, the stained glass windows, of the Resurrection over here and here's Jonah climbing out of the big fish right over here. We need to understand one in terms of the other. The Jonah story is not complete without the Jesus story, and the Jesus story is better understood if you have the Jonah antecedent.

Herzman: Well, what we are going to do now is make the outrageous case that Dante writes his own poem in imitation of the Bible. Not simply that he uses stories from the Bible, which he does; not simply that he uses characters from the Bible, which he does— the pilgrim is going to meet a bunch of them, and chat with them in some cases; not simply that he gives the Bible this special place, but he's writing in imitation of the Bible in the fundamental sense that, just as the Bible proceeds according to this typological way in which an event is related to other events and can't really be understood except in terms of those other events, so also with his poem, that one way to state it is that you can't really understand anything that happens in the beginning of the poem, let's say in the first part, in the Inferno, without fully understanding what comes next in the Purgatorio and in the Paradiso. There are events and characters in the latter parts of the poem, which refer back to—and complete things that happen—earlier on.

Cook: Dante has a number of ways of helping us to do that. The mistake a lot of readers make, I think, especially those who only read the Inferno, is assuming that if they've read the Inferno they've really got down Dante's point of view, his understanding of everything. They know what he thinks about this political issue or this moral issue, or whatever, and of course what they miss is exactly what Ron's describing, because, just as in Scripture, the same issues, if you will, come up again and again and again, and we get a number of different ways to look at them either within the Old Testament or in the New Testament, or between the two Testaments so similarly that we really need to get to the end. In fact, one of the great lines of Dante's scholarship is, when you've finished reading the poem, you're ready to read the poem.

Herzman: Another one of the lines is that Dante expects us to take this poem as though it had the same kind of historical reality that Scripture does. Think about that for a minute. As we said earlier, one of the things that made Scripture so important is that for the Christian it is the record of God's actions in history—that it was not a text self-contained but it was a text that spoke to, and about, actions that really happened. Now, most of us don't believe that Dante really did take this trip to the afterlife. There are some exceptions to that. I was reading an essay by somebody the other day who said she was, in fact, taught by somebody who believed fully that Dante really did take that trip. I guess you're allowed to do that, and in some of our more extravagant moments we're sympathetic to that perspective, but for the most part we think that this is a fiction that Dante invented about the journey of a character named Dante to the afterlife, but, in one of the great one-liners of Dante criticism and scholarship of the 20th century, the great fiction of the poem is that it's not a fiction. That is to say, Dante wants us to take it with the same kind of seriousness as we would take biblical events that really did happen. In other words, to suspend our disbelief and to see Dante the pilgrim on this journey to the afterlife, and to see that this journey is modeled on that movement from creation to judgment that is in Scripture, or some of the other important journey motifs in Scripture, perhaps most important that of the Exodus.

Cook: If we now turn to some specific parts of the Old Testament especially, because they are perhaps less obviously appliable to Dante, who is a Christian, than the New Testament text, the best place to start is the Exodus. This story, which really takes up four books of the Old Testament, is referred to constantly and retold in the Psalms and other places. It's, of course, in the literal sense, the journey of the Hebrews from Egypt to Palestine. They get out by going through the Red Sea. They get into Palestine by going through the Jordan [River], but as soon as we say that, we've only begun the story of the Exodus, as we know today as Americans. We know for example how black slaves in the South used the story of the Exodus, and not only saw it as an allegory, but also saw it sometimes as almost literally a guide to the Ohio River. So that we find too in Dante, it's not just a story, although it is that. It is also the journey from exile to homeland, from bondage to freedom, from death to life. It is a paradigmatic story of the Hebrews, and Dante fully understands and uses it.

Herzman: So, just to sort of piggyback on that, or to apply Exodus to the poem, it makes sense, it really is a good way to look at the poem, to see the Inferno as equivalent to the bondage of Egypt, the Purgatorio as the wandering in the desert, the Paradiso as reaching the promised land. It's also equally important to say really what it's about is this physical actual geography, but it's also about this internal turn from slavery to freedom, and so, as far as Dante the pilgrim himself is concerned, the Exodus provides the model from slavery to freedom, okay? Dante writes a poem about a guy named Dante who starts out dumb and who ends up smart, but it's not dumb and smart in simply intellectual or a cognitive sense, it's spiritually dumb ending up spiritually smart, or spiritually enslaved and ends up spiritually free, so that the whole Exodus motif deals with the poem he set up, but also, and perhaps even more important, the nature of the journey that he's taking. Dante is, in his own life in the poem, reenacting the Exodus.

Cook: We also want to turn to another hunk of the Old Testament for its particular importance to Dante, and that is the 22 books that are labeled the "Prophetic Books," in particular, the 16 books that we call the "Writing Prophets." Now, today, sometimes we have a debased notion of what prophecy means, reading tea leaves or whatever, but my one-liner about Old Testament prophets would be this: Although they are dramatically and intensely concerned with the future, they are deeply, deeply rooted in their past. In other words, if you will, God has a track record. They are very, very careful observers of the present, and only when they've done those things do they really talk in ways that are powerful about the future. It's not guessing; it's not tealeaves; it is a prophet who is a rooted in the past, and a careful observer of the present, and therefore can talk intelligently and powerfully about the future.

Herzman: You'll notice in many examples of prophecy in Hebrew Scripture in the Old Testament, one of the things that enables them to do it is that they are given some kind of God's-eye view of things, and they are able to immerse themselves in the present, through the past, and therefore it's almost as though the future is part of this whole continuum. If you begin thinking about that in terms of Dante, it's sort of interesting to see how Dante himself, of course, has this God's-eye view of things because he is taking a journey to realms of experience that are not usually allotted to us in this life. He goes to the three parts of the afterlife. Well, that gives him a perspective that others don't have. It enables him to see what others don't see, but of course, he takes that perspective and he applies it exactly in the manner of the Old Testament prophets to the events of the present time, and so I think the case that we want to make as strongly as possible is that Dante acts as a kind of prophetic commentator on the events of his own time. Even as he is very interested in other events and other times, he wants us, in other words, to see him incorporating the spirit of biblical prophecy into the *Commedia* itself.

Cook: I think we can sort of end this section by saying just a couple other things. First of all, today one of the phrases we use for prophets is they speak truth to power. Dante has to learn if he's going to himself speak prophetically, that you have to tell the truth no matter who it might hurt. You've got to tell the truth no matter how much damage the people you tell the truth about can do to you, and that's a very tough lesson, and Dante not only needs to learn that in the abstract, he learns it from the prophets in the concrete. Just follow the story of Jeremiah. He's booted around, he's arrested, he's thrown in a hole, because he doesn't have a lot of good news and kings don't like not-good-news, and so Dante can not only model prophecy as a form of speaking, he can also model the prophets' life in his own exile and the experience of exile.

Herzman: So, essentially, it's the exile that demands that he begin thinking about things as a prophet would, and that means that his job is to speak to power and to speak to the abuses of power. Well, where does he do that? In the poem itself. One very important way of taking a look at the *Divine Comedy* is it was meant to speak to power and to talk about the abuses of power, and, like Jeremiah and the other Old Testament prophets, Dante is somebody who comes to this through the experience of exile. That exile, too, was the condition that Jeremiah and the other prophets had to face. So, Dante is saying, well, this condition can be a way of speaking truth to power without regard to the consequences. One way to take a look at that, Dante is able to write the poem from the point of view of somebody who doesn't have a whole heck of a lot more to lose. He can afford to speak the truth. So, that prophetic strain is something that we would say is deep and consistent throughout the entire *Commedia*.

Cook: While we will argue that if you have to say pick out one text from the past and put them all in order, which one did Dante use the most, or value the most, I think we both agree that it's the Bible, but it's not the only text, because Dante, like the Middle Ages in general, is the heir also of the classical tradition, the Greek and Roman tradition, with its myths, with its philosophy, with its literature, with its history, and therefore we want to turn now, at the end of this lecture and continue into the next lecture saying a little bit about one classical figure of paramount importance, one that strikes us right in Canto 1 because the first person we really meet other than Dante, the pilgrim himself, is in fact not a Christian, not a biblical figure, but a figure from classical antiquity, a poet named Virgil

Herzman: Virgil shows up very early in the poem. He stays for quite a long time. It turns out that Virgil is Dante's guide for fully two-thirds of the poem. He gives way to Beatrice, remember we mentioned her in the first lecture as the subject for Dante's early love poetry. Virgil gives way only at the very end of the Purgatorio, so for two-thirds of the poem he is the one who guides Dante through the afterlife, and it turns out that, not surprisingly, his great epic poem, the *Aeneid*, was a model for Dante in constructing his own poem, a source for a great many of the episodes that are in Dante's poem, as well as a great many of the characters that are in the poem, and also, occasionally, a kind of rival to Dante in the sense that there are things in Virgil that Dante thinks about, and that Dante sort of works on, and that Dante redoes and rewrites. He's sort of not satisfied with the answers that Virgil comes up with in his own poem. So, one of the things that I think we would like to come away with in this lecture is the sense that even though the influence of the Bible is clearly paramount to Dante, Virgil represents something that balances it, in a way. That the way in which the *Aeneid* is used in the poem has this same kind of generating and generative force in the poem that the Bible does.

Cook: Perhaps it is worthwhile to just remind ourselves of a little bit of history. Virgil was born in 70 B.C. in what we would call the late

Roman Republic, and he died in 19 B.C. during the reign of the Emperor Augustus, and in this great poem, the *Aeneid*, he wrote things other than the *Aeneid*, is, in fact, the story of the founding of Rome beginning with the fall of Troy and ending with Aeneas coming to Italy and sort of winning the battles that needed to be won, to establish Trojan blood in Italy once and for all. The story itself is important. The episodes and the characters of it are, perhaps, even more important for what Dante is going to be doing in the *Commedia*.

Herzman: So, that's where we will pick it up with the next lecture.

Lecture Four
Literary Antecedents, II

Scope:

This lecture continues the discussion of Dante's use of earlier literature. We continue the discussion of Virgil's *Aeneid*, emphasizing both the political and personal concerns of Virgil that become the concerns of Dante. The next work we discuss is Augustine's spiritual autobiography, the *Confessions*, which provides for Dante the model of a first-person narrator and, like Dante's poem, attempts to synthesize the biblical and the classical traditions. Finally, we take a look at Dante's own earlier writings, from which he also draws in the *Commedia*. In particular, we examine how he makes use of his own earlier poetic, political, and philosophical writings.

Outline

I. The *Aeneid* (comparable but not quite equal to the Bible as a source for Dante) deals with concerns that Dante found both politically and personally central.

II. In Book II, for example, we see how the story of Troy contains the seed of Roman history.

   A. We learn that the idea of *empire* has a "direction," from East to West, from defeat to victory, from tragic loss to newfound land. In some sense, then, the *Aeneid* is a secular analogue to the biblical story of Exodus.

   B. For Dante, the story of that empire continues to his own day. Rome's history is Dante's history.

   C. Rome's world empire governed well and provides a good model—the Church's being "headquartered" in Rome is providential.

III. In Book IV, which tells of Aeneas and Dido, we learn how a love story helps define what it means to be a Roman.

   A. Dante projects this story onto the *Commedia*.

   B. Dido is a character in Dante's Inferno.

      1. She is an example of a sinner who submits reason to desire.

    2. She is given a different place in Dante's afterlife than in Virgil's.

    3. She is an example of how Dante is not afraid to revise Virgil's poem.

C. Dante is aware of the story of Dido and Aeneas when he writes the story of Dante and Beatrice.

    1. Virgil suggests that love and duty are not compatible.

        a. While Dido, the queen, dallies with Aeneas, the city is neglected.

        b. Aeneas must press forward on his mission; Dido, jilted, commits suicide.

    2. Dante suggests that love and duty can be compatible.

D. Aeneas's ability to recover after his mistakes suggests a positive model for Dante the pilgrim. Dido, the despairing suicide, is a negative example.

IV. Book VI of the *Aeneid* is the trip to the underworld.

    A. Much of Dante's geography is taken from Virgil.

    B. So is the sense that one gets the kind of afterlife one deserves.

    C. Dante uses many specific incidents in *Aeneid* VI.

        1. Aeneas's meeting in the afterworld with his father's shade is crucial to his renewed sense of vocation.

        2. Dante needs a similar ancestor-driven renewal from his own trip to the afterworld.

V. Another major literary influence on Dante is Augustine's *Confessions*.

    A. Like Dante, Augustine (354–430 C.E.) attempts to fuse the biblical and classical traditions.

    B. Like Dante, Augustine makes use of the Bible and of Virgil, as well.

    C. In writing his own spiritual autobiography, Augustine provides Dante with the model for writing about himself.

        1. As he did with Virgil, Dante will "correct" or rewrite Augustine at times.

        2. Because Dante, unlike Augustine, writes at a time when Christianity has become secure as the established religion, Dante can be more "generous" to the pagan classics.

D. Both the *Confessions* and the *Commedia* can be read as spiritual autobiographies.

VI. Dante also draws from the earlier works of the Roman poet Statius and the early Christian historian Orosius.

Readings:

Augustine, *The Confessions*, Books 7, 8.

Virgil, *The Aeneid of Virgil*, Books 2, 4, 6.

Questions to Consider:

1. Does it make any sense for Dante to so carefully model the Christian afterlife on the pagan afterlife of the *Aeneid*?

2. How is Dante's autobiographical poem dependent on the first great work of Christian biography, Augustine's *Confessions*?

3. If Dante makes such great use of the *Confessions*, why doesn't the poet tell us that directly somewhere in the *Commedia*?

Lecture Four—Transcript
Literary Antecedents, II

Cook: The story of Troy and its fall is one of the most famous stories in all of Western literature. Most of us first engaged it by reading the *Iliad* and/or the *Odyssey* of Homer. It's important to say that Dante had not read those poems because they did not exist in a translation into a language, Latin for example, that Dante could read. He knew the plots, but he had not read Homer, and therefore we need to remember that for Dante, first and foremost, the story of the fall of Troy is a story that is recorded in the great epic poem of the Latin tradition, Virgil's *Aeneid*, and therefore, going back and claiming all that story, as well as the artistry, of Virgil as his own is an important element in understanding how Dante came to write this poem.

Herzman: I guess that we would argue that going back to Troy, for Dante, going back to what for him was the source of many important things in his world view is, while not as important as going back to the Bible, meant to be seen almost on equal footing with it. So, we're suggesting then that the *Aeneid* contains both political and perhaps even personal concerns that are central to Dante in the *Commedia*. Now, what we're going to do is sort of talk a little bit about them in sort of specific terms, keeping in mind always that we're going to be leaving a lot out. This was a poem that Dante knew probably for the most part by heart, and again, as we talked earlier with Dante's knowledge of the biblical tradition, the fact that Dante knew the Bible in a way and at a depth that is foreign to us in our own time, equally true with the classical tradition. He knew Virgil and he knew Virgil's poem, the *Aeneid*, in a way that would be sort of astonishing to us. So, we're going to talk a little bit first about Troy and what that would mean to Dante. First of all, the most important thing to say for him was that the story of Troy for Dante was about the seed of Roman history and Roman history turns out to be Dante's own history.

Cook: We need to ask why. First of all, remember that Dante lives in Italy, but more than that, Dante looks back to the days of the Roman Empire (when Virgil writes his poem on other things) as a time when the world really was well governed, because for Dante, when you had a world empire—for Dante, essentially the Roman Empire was a world empire—when you have a world empire it provides the opportunity for greater justice, less competition. Again, remember in

Florence the big issue is competition. The city-states around Florence, the issue is competition, how do you eliminate the downside of competition? Well, Dante believed in the idea of Rome, and that the Roman Empire was itself a model from the past, a model that had a great deal to say to the present. But that's only half the story, maybe even a little bit less than half, because while today we might say the fact that the Roman Catholic Church has its "headquarters" in Rome is essentially accidental. For Dante it was providential. There's no accidental nature to the fact that on the one hand Rome was the center of the Roman Empire, and on the other hand Rome was the center of the Church, that God chose Rome for these dual roles, and in Dante's own day the Roman emperors, now living in Germany, had abandoned Rome, and the popes were perverting what their job was in Rome. So, when Dante looked back, he goes all the way back to creation in the Bible to the creation of Rome, and that story is the *Aeneid* story.

Herzman: Of course, it starts really in Book II of the *Aeneid* when we see the destruction of Troy, the story of the Trojan Horse, the burning of Troy, the successful attempt of Aeneas and some of his followers to leave Troy, that is the beginning of a journey that goes all the way to the founding of Rome. For Dante, it would not end with the founding of Rome; it's the Roman Empire and it's the Church, so that in a very real way what we see in the story of Book II of the *Aeneid* is the seed of Dante's own history, a story that continues down to his own day, and not surprisingly, a great number of the characters from Book II of the *Aeneid* emerge from time to time as characters in the *Commedia,* but, of course, in the background is always the journey of Aeneas himself, that if he is making this journey from Troy to what ultimately is going to become Rome, he is going in the "direction" of *empire* from East to West; he's going from defeat to victory; he's going from tragic loss to new land. In some ways that too becomes a parallel for Dante's own journey in the afterlife, through hell and purgatory and heaven. In other words, it becomes a kind of classical—we would use the word, I'm not sure Dante would—secular analog of the Exodus story, and so in some ways we have to say that Dante's journey piggybacks onto the journey of Aeneas and can't be really understood without understanding that other journey.

Cook: It was a rough journey; it was a tough journey; and it was a journey where there was also some sidetracking. It isn't that Aeneas made a beeline from Troy to Italy, it was in many ways a morally, a physically, and in other ways a rocky road just as the Hebrews wandered for 40 years in the desert before they crossed to Jordan and entered the promised land. So, the parallels, although not exact, are very important, and the more we abstract the story the more clear the parallels become.

Herzman: If we're talking about sidetracking, the most important of those sidetracks, it seems to me, is the story of Aeneas and Dido that takes place in Book IV for the most part, but is also throughout much of the rest of the *Aeneid* as well. It's a love story, which Virgil's audience would have seen as something that helped to define what it means to be a Roman. Basically, Dido and Aeneas meet in Carthage; they fall in love, sort of a euphemistic term for what they do; they horse around for a while, and Aeneas is visited by Mercury who says, "Uh, uh, you can't do this. Remember you've got this duty, this mission," and so he leaves because he realizes that it is important for him to subordinate his own personal desires, to subordinate his sort of hanky-panky with Dido to his greater duty. So it becomes this story of duty winning out over passion, and as such it becomes a story that essentially spoke to the Romans' own sense of duty, own sense of what it is, what it means, what is needed, what is necessary to run an empire, but it also becomes a story that continues in its afterlife as others sort of pick it up and use it again and again, and in particular, in Dante's own *Commedia*. We've already mentioned that Aeneas is a character, but so also is Dido herself. We see her as one of the sinners in Inferno among the lustful, and her sin, like the others who are there, was somebody who submitted reason to desire.

Now, a couple of things are interesting about that. First of all, it means that Dante actually gave Dido a little bit of a different place in the afterlife than what she had in Virgil's poem. She's in the afterlife in Virgil's poem, but basically in a better place with her first husband. Dante is not afraid to put her among those who are punished in the circle of the lustful, and I want to use this example just simply to point out that Dante is not afraid to revise Virgil and revise Virgil's poem when it suits his own purposes. That is to say that what he has done is sort of come to a place where he and Virgil disagree. So, he is aware of this story of Dido and Aeneas, and he uses it there, but he also uses it when he tells the story of Dante and Beatrice. In other words, one way to take a look at what happens in the Dante/Beatrice story is to see this as sort of Dante's rewriting in a very broad sense of the story of Aeneas and Dido. That is to say, if you look at the story as Virgil tells it, one of the hard lessons that Virgil is teaching here is that somehow passionate love and duty are not really compatible. You can have one; you can have the other; you can't have both. Dante, at least in the story of himself, the pilgrim and Beatrice, is an attempt, I think, for him to re-explore that possibility, to possibly rewrite the ending, and you see, therefore, that Dante is not simply using the specific characters in a narrow sense, but the larger idea that is represented by this story in a larger sense.

Cook: It's worthwhile also saying this about Dido: We haven't really introduced you to her and said who she is. She turns out to be the Queen of Carthage, which is, again, an independent nation at the time this story is allegedly set, and you need to know a couple of things about her. First of all, queens have obligations. She's in charge of the country. Secondly, her first husband has died, and she took an oath not to be unfaithful, to be, in fact, faithful to the ashes of her husband, Sichaeus. So she doesn't come to us with a blank slate, she comes with a story and a set of obligations, and as Virgil tells the story of Dido and Aeneas sort of romping around for a while, he stops and gives us a glimpse of the city of Carthage, and he says, you know, nobody is manning the towers of the city, nobody is repairing the walls of the city. That's, after all, something that the queen does. So, even though Dido and Aeneas are having a good old time, the fact is she has duties, too, and she's unfaithful to those obligations, and the consequences are extraordinary. They are extraordinary to the city of Carthage, and they are extraordinary to her because when Aeneas listens to Mercury and heads off to Italy, Dido commits suicide, and therefore we see this tragedy that seems to have begun with a kind of love/passion that has been damaging to the individual involved and to the city of Carthage.

Herzman: Now, notice in that what Virgil is trying to do, of course, is contrast Dido with Aeneas. They both make mistakes. Dido doesn't quite know how to recover and kills herself out of passion and actually passion and hatred. Aeneas's ability to recover after his mistakes sort of sets up another way in which he's a model for Dante's journey, because, of course, Dante's journey starts when he is lost in a dark wood, and the whole process, really, of his development in the poem is learning how to get out of that dark wood, which I think is very much related to this notion of learning how to recover from mistakes that you have already made.

Cook: Perhaps the part of the *Aeneid* that is most directly applied by Dante in the *Commedia* is the journey Aeneas takes in Book VI, because in Book VI Aeneas goes to the underworld, and he meets the shades of those who have died. Dido, as Ron suggested, among them, and while he is there he not only gets to chat with some folks who have been dead, but he also gets to hear words that tell about Rome's destiny and Rome's greatness. It brings the past and the future together as he journeys to the underworld. As Dante says at the beginning of Inferno 2 when Virgil proposes to him, "Let's go to the underworld," one of Dante's first reactions is, "Wait a minute, I know Aeneas did that but I'm not Aeneas." As Ron has already hinted, in some ways Dante does become Aeneas.

Herzman: It's interesting also in that regard, we've talked a little bit then about major episodes in the *Aeneid*, the fall of Troy, the hanky-panky with Dido, the trip to the underworld, the trip to the underworld is the one that really gets the double asterisk mark of approval here because if you go back to the central question, "Why is it that Virgil is the one who guides Dante through two-thirds of the poem?" one answer is he's a guy who knows the territory. That is to say, through his writing about the underworld he has kind of staked out a claim to be Dante's guide. You want somebody who knows the territory, who knows it better than this guy who has described it so imaginatively in Book VI of the *Aeneid*, and, in fact, if you take a look at that Book VI with some care, you see that a great deal of the geography that Virgil invents, really, turns out to be geography that Dante himself uses in the Inferno, that he is somebody who borrows pretty massively at that point. So, also, it's interesting that there is this sense it's not developed with any degree of exactness, but there's this sense from Book VI of the *Aeneid* that folks get the kind of afterlife that they deserve. We think of that in terms of Dante's incorporation into his poem as something that came from the Christian tradition, but, in fact, Dante was able to get something like that from the classical tradition as well. So, Virgil becomes this figure of overwhelming importance because of what Virgil already achieved.

Cook: So as we journey down into hell we're going to cross strangely named rivers, we're going to meet some folks, and we're going to understand a lot of that geography specifically because it is borrowed from the *Aeneid* VI. If you want, other than looking at a drawing of hell in a translation of Dante, if you want a glimpse of something that will give you a kind of roadmap, inexact though it may be, do a little Virgil review. Before you take your journey by reading Dante's Inferno and it will pay off, if nothing else, simply in the way, as you read the notes then that accompany your translation, they'll make a lot more sense. You'll have something to grab a hold of, and you will be able to see how much Dante draws from this Virgilian description of the afterlife.

Herzman: To sum up, one of the things that is very interesting about Aeneas's own trip is that he takes this journey to the underworld because he wants to see his father who is there, this great act of loyalty, but also because he needs an answer to why he should continue, why he should go on, that in Aeneas you have somebody for whom life has not been a walk in the park. He has lost his wife; he has lost his city; he's in exile; he's going from place to place, blown ashore, losing men, losing his father, and this sense of "Why go on?" seems to become more and more of a question for him. Going down to the underworld he gets to see a picture of Roman greatness that allows him to continue because it basically says, "Look, you're the one who can bring this about," or, "If you don't, if you don't continue, this greatness is never going to take place." So, he comes out from the underworld with a renewed sense of vocation, if you will. Notice that if you apply that general idea to the *Commedia* it works very well. Dante takes the trip to the afterlife to figure out what it is all about. In the terms that we've been using, to get him out of this dark wood, this dark wood of error that he is in, and so like Virgil, he's got to go down so that he can come up. Again, something that fits very nicely in the Christian tradition also has this classical analog.

Cook: As a final illustration of a point we've made before, and we'll make again and again as we walk through and journey with Dante in the *Commedia* is that, for example, Dante does meet his ancestor in the afterlife and had a very long conversation and found out why he has to go back after this journey and do something important. He doesn't meet him in hell; he doesn't meet him in purgatory; he meets him in heaven. You'd never have a feel for that part of the Virgilian parallel if you only read the Inferno. We've got to go all the way through, because it's only in heaven that Dante has a sort of parallel conversation with his ancestor, in this case not his father but his great, great grandfather.

Herzman: We're going to just shift gears slightly now and talk about a third influence—the Bible, Virgil, and now a text written by Saint Augustine called the *Confessions*, which also is very important for giving you a feel for how Dante uses previous literary text. *Confessions* written by Saint Augustine, and before we tell you a little bit about the text, maybe we need to tell you a little bit about Augustine himself.

Cook: Saint Augustine was born in North Africa in 354 at about the time Christianity is at a transitional period from a persecuted religion to a dominant religion in the Roman Empire. In fact, his own family sort of personifies that struggle. One parent was pagan; one parent was Christian. Then, at the age of about 31, after many years of struggle, Augustine converted to Christianity in Italy. By this time he had come to Italy, and, in fact, that conversion and his baptism took place in Milan. Shortly after that time he went back to North Africa, where he became the bishop of the city of Hippo, which is in modern Algeria, and there he died in the year 430. He was one of the most voluminous authors in the entire history of Christianity, writing sermons and letters and biblical commentaries and a 1,000-page book called *The City of God,* all of which were vitally important and were well known in the Middle Ages as well as now. But especially for the purposes of the *Commedia*, the work that is most personal and immediate to Dante is this story of his own life up through his conversion, the story that is called *Confessions*, written when he was in his mid-forties, that is to say, basically a decade after his conversion.

Herzman: First of all, it's important to just sort of stake out the obvious similarity, and that is that Augustine, in writing *Confessions,* is writing about himself. In the previous epic literary tradition we have Virgil writing about Aeneas; we'll talk a little bit about Homer, Homer writes about Achilles, and he writes about Odysseus, and what you have in Dante is the writing of a poem in that same epic tradition but the hero of Dante's poem is Dante. The Dante pilgrim is sort of modeled on the Augustine who is the subject of *Confessions* even as Augustine the converted bishop looks back at his early life and tells us about it. You have the poet telling us about this Dante of 1300, even though the poet himself is living and writing at a much later time. So, the idea of writing about the self and writing about the self in terms of a kind of spiritual autobiography turns out to be extremely important in the *Commedia*. Among the other things we can say about it: What is this work? What is this great epic that Dante writes? It is a spiritual autobiography.

Cook: I would describe the narrative part—not all 13 books are narrative—but I would describe the narrative part as beginning with the problem, what I would call the "mis-education" of Augustine both in school and from his parents, and then when Augustine decides at about the age of 18 to get serious about life, to learn and to seek things beyond immediate physical gratification. Boy is that hard. He has a lot to unlearn, as well as a lot to learn, and even as he grows in his struggle, he falls back from time to time, even as he grows in his struggle, it is very hard to get rid of those old habits. It has simply become a part of who he is, and so in several books, I would say Books 3 to 7 of *Confessions*, we struggled for Augustine to really understand well enough. But, we all know that understanding isn't enough. You ask people, "Did you know you were doing something wrong?" Most of the time they say, "Yes." The problem isn't intellect, the problem is will, and therefore this most beautiful book, for me, the eighth book, we have the struggle where Augustine is fighting the fact that he knows what he should do, but can't choose it because it means leaving so many things that have given him pleasure behind, and as it leads to its dramatic conclusion at the end of Book 8, he's in a garden under a tree, he's called to pick up a book, he picks up the words of Saint Paul in the Letter to the Romans. Here's the call to put away nature and nature's appetite and rely on God. He doesn't have to read beyond that. He puts the book down, he gets filled full of confidence. He has, in fact, made his choice, and think about that in parallel to Dante, being really confused, struggling to learn things you need to learn and unlearn things that need to be unlearned, and then finally coming to this dramatic choice, and ultimately making that choice.

Herzman: It's also interesting that Augustine tells the story of his own conversion, and we might ask, "Well, before he was a Christian what was he?" He was, I guess, a kind of pagan, and he was somebody who was educated in the pagan classics, in classical literature in particular. His profession, he was a professor of rhetoric, I guess the equivalent would be he would be teaching at Harvard Law School if he were alive and well now, and what he grew up with were the great works of classical literature, and at a certain point he says, "You know, what I need to do is find truth, and I'm not getting it there." So, *Confessions* turns out to be this intense search for truth that ultimately leads to Christianity, but before he gets there, before he gets there he says, "Tried a lot of things, didn't work, found something that was really very helpful." In Book 7, he talks about finding the Platonist philosophers, as he calls them, philosophers, in the Greek tradition following Plato, who taught him basic truths that were necessary for his conversion to Christianity. So, Augustine becomes a model of somebody who is of two traditions really, of the classical and of the biblical or Christian, and *Confessions* is an attempt to sort of see how these works fit together, and in exactly the same way you could argue that the *Commedia* is an attempt to see how the classical and the Christian traditions fit together. Dante, who is inspired and energized by the Bible, but for whom Virgil is the guide. Virgil operates for Dante in much the same way the Platonist philosophers are a guide to Augustine.

Cook: I would also make the point (just as Ron has pointed out) that Dante does not hesitate to fix up or "correct" Virgil in some ways, so I think that is true with Augustine in this sense in particular. When Augustine is writing, various kinds of pagan theologies and philosophies were real alternatives to people. That is to say, in fact, probably Christians were barely a majority, if that, during most of Augustine's life. There were other real alternatives, and therefore, although Augustine is very deeply indebted to the classics, and he says so and is very open about it, he's also a little bit nervous about how the classics can be misused, lead people the wrong way, become things in and for themselves, and so in some of his writings he sometimes sounds a little bit harsher about the classics than we might expect, given what Ron has said, quite accurately. Dante lives in a different world. Christianity is the universal religion of the place that Dante lives, that is to say, in Europe in the 13th century, and nobody is going to go off and start a cult of Jupiter, or whatever, and therefore, in a sense, Dante can be more "generous" in the way that he uses the classics. He doesn't have to be quite so worried that the classics are going to be leading people off in a direction that takes them in opposition to Christianity, and therefore in some sense his synthesis is more complete than Augustine's, of course it helps that he lives 900 years later and has a lot of intervening tradition to guide him in that direction.

Herzman: One example that proves Bill's point is that early on Augustine talks about what turned out to have been a schoolboy text for him; he was reading Virgil's *Aeneid*. He says, "I read this and I read the story about this Dido person, and I began weeping for Dido's plight," and then he has this sort of wonderful passage about "Why was I weeping for Dido and not weeping for my own sins," and talks about the fact that he was clearly reading Virgil for the wrong reasons, and this sense therefore that in some ways Virgil was a kind of dangerous document. Now, there are other ways in which Augustine is perhaps a little bit more sympathetic to Virgil, but you get the sense that he was always a little bit iffy about what Virgil's place was in his own education. Nothing like that is true for Dante. For Dante, Virgil is the master who taught him about poetry and who also had a whole lot of other things to teach him about virtue, about the very sorts of things the poem itself is concerned with, finding the good life. Where Augustine sees somebody who is a danger, Dante sees somebody who is a guide.

Cook: The last point I would make is that remember, again, Augustine lives 900 years before Dante, and Dante therefore has a lot of intervening tradition that, alas, we don't have time to talk about. There are also a lot of classical figures that were very well known to Dante, whose reputation has slipped somewhat in the modern world. The epic poet Statius would be an example of a pagan. The Christian historian Orosius, a disciple of Augustine, would be another example of that. Therefore, Dante's biblical, classical, and post-classical world of sorts is much bigger. We've only begun to suggest that, but now it's time to begin our journey with Dante.

Lecture Five
"Abandon Every Hope, All You Who Enter"

Scope:

This lecture provides an introduction to hell and the beginning of the pilgrim's journey. Hell is the realm of the afterlife in which unrepentant sinners dwell. The geography of hell can be thought of as a physical and moral geography in which successive concentric circles reveal the nature of ever more serious sins. Dante's journey through hell, under the guidance of Virgil, takes him more deeply into the realm of evil. The major divisions of hell, very carefully structured by the poet, are taken from classical sources. The three large categories of moral failure—incontinence, violence, and fraud—represent the inversion of the classical virtues of moderation, courage, and wisdom.

The journey begins with the pilgrim in a dark wood of error. As he is about to abandon his attempt to climb out of this condition, he is met by the poet Virgil, who tells him that he must go by another route if he is to get out of his condition. In Canto 2, Dante shows his reluctance to take the journey. Virgil convinces him of the necessity of making it by telling Dante about a chain of heavenly ladies who have come to aid him. In Canto 3, Dante passes through the famous gates of hell and finds himself in the company of those who refused to make moral choices while on earth. In Canto 4, Dante is with the virtuous pagans, those figures who lived without benefit of Christian baptism. Each of these cantos helps the reader understand the nature of Dante's afterlife.

Outline

I. Hell is the place where unrepentant sinners dwell.

   A. It consists of concentric circles inside the earth, each smaller than the previous one.

   B. The geography of hell is a moral geography as well as a physical one, reflecting the nature of the sin.

   C. The nature of the sin is made clear by Dante the pilgrim's dramatic encounters with the sinners.

II. Hell is divided into three major categories of moral failure: incontinence, violence, and fraud.

    A. These divisions are inversions of the classical virtues of moderation, courage, and wisdom.

    B. The fourth classical virtue, justice, is also reflected in hell: The poet is constructing an unjust city.

    C. The deeper Dante journeys, the more serious the sin he encounters.

III. The sinners that Dante meets are from many times and places.

    A. Some are great figures from history, literature, or myth.

    B. Some are "local" figures who would have faded into oblivion except for Dante's treatment of them.

    C. Thus, Dante combines the universal and the local.

    D. The sinners have in common a desire to justify themselves and to put the blame for their actions elsewhere.

IV. Dante the pilgrim must learn to view the sinner from a different perspective than that of the sinners themselves.

    A. The sinners all lack self-knowledge.

    B. They have lost the "good of intellect," as Virgil tells the pilgrim.

V. The nature of hell unfolds, though only somewhat gradually in the opening cantos.

    A. Canto 1 shows the pilgrim, "midway along the journey of our life," caught in a dark wood (*selva oscura*) of error.

        1. Three beasts impede his progress out of the dark wood.

        2. He is rescued by the appearance of the poet Virgil.

    B. Canto 2 shows the pilgrim negotiating with Virgil about the nature of the journey.

        1. Virgil tells the poet about three blessed ladies who have made his help possible: the Virgin Mary, Saint Lucy, and Beatrice.

        2. The journey is not a reward for Dante but a last-ditch effort to save him from his spiritual disorientation.

C. Canto 3 shows the pilgrim passing through the gates of hell.

   1. Hell's inscription is a clue to what happens there.

   2. Dante finds himself in the vestibule of hell, where he encounters those who refused to make choices while on earth.

   3. These "sinners" get what they deserve: they chase banners for eternity; they are never named.

D. In Canto 4, the pilgrim encounters the virtuous pagans.

   1. Dante meets great figures from antiquity here.

   2. The only punishment here is separation from God.

   3. We learn of the necessity of baptism for salvation.

   4. We learn that this place was also the abode for Old Testament figures who were led out by Christ at the "Harrowing of Hell."

   a. Christ's journey, during the Easter Triduum, down into hell, then up to risen life, is the model for Dante's journey.

   b. Like Christ, Dante will make a descent that is meant to lead people out of hell or off the hell-bound trail.

Readings:

Dante, *Inferno*, Cantos 1–4.

John Freccero, *Dante: The Poetics of Conversion*, Chapters 1–2.

Questions to Consider:

1. How does Dante's predicament help us to understand how we have gone astray from a path we meant to follow?

2. How does God show grace to Dante in a way that is "tailored" to the pilgrim's needs?

Lecture Five—Transcript
"Abandon Every Hope, All You Who Enter"

Herzman: In the lectures that we've done so far we've tried to give you as much background as we could about the nature of the poem so that when we take the journey along with Dante the pilgrim, we will be well equipped. Well, today we start that journey, and we start it by going directly to hell, and pretty much what we'd like to do for our journey is to go along with the pilgrim and as he learns things in the process, so too will we. But, we do need a little bit of a map to orient ourselves as well. You may remember that in an earlier lecture we mentioned that in order to be a member of Dante's afterlife, it was necessary to be dead, and to be dead by the year 1300. What we want to do now is to suggest that you need something else to be a member of the afterlife Part one, hell. When we ask this to our students, "What do you need to be a member of the afterlife in hell?" inevitably a lot of hands go up, and they say, "You need to be a sinner," and we say, "Yes, that's true, but that's only part of the answer. There's another part that is equally important." They think for a while, occasionally somebody gets it. You have to be a sinner who is unrepentant. Now it's important to see that in terms of what happens in other parts of the *Commedia* because the people that we meet there too, some of them were sinners and some of them were pretty famous at sinning, but they did repent and that makes all of the difference. So, it's important for what we see later on, but it's also very important for what we're going to see in hell because the whole idea of not being repentant really does determine the way all of these characters are going to interact with Dante. So, we start off then by saying we're going to a place with the pilgrim where Dante's going to meet unrepentant sinners.

Cook: We need to say a word about the geography of hell. Where is it that we're actually going in this journey? Well, for one thing, we're going down to the center of the earth. Don't worry, in Dante's day no educated person thought the world was flat, so if you learned that about Columbus in 1492, we've got to get this out of our heads because people from the ancient Greeks on knew better. So, at any rate—we're going to go down though a series of concentric circles in a highly articulated design that Dante creates. In fact, we're going to go through nine circles of hell, and as much as it sounds like, as we read Dante's description, he's describing a real place and giving us a lot of details; this sort of reminds me of that back on earth. We also need to remember that it's not just a physical geography; it's a moral geography. As we journey toward the bottom of hell, toward the center of the earth, where we meet Satan, the sinners and the sins are more serious. Furthermore, when we read those descriptions of the various tortures and punishments, don't just see them as what new idea can Dante come up with that's a little grosser than the last one? That would be a totally wrong way to approach it, but rather how can we read the geography and the punishments as a way of understanding the very nature of the sin that this person has committed, and as Ron said, not repented.

Herzman: Again, in terms of the kind of major contours of hell, Dante deals with three separate kinds of moral failure that he names incontinence, violence, and fraud. There are a lot of different ways to think about this. To me, the most useful—and in many ways the most convenient—is to think about it as a kind of inversion of the classical virtues of moderation of courage and of wisdom, so that the inversion of the virtue of moderation is incontinence. We'll find out later that the one-line definition of that is subjecting reason to desire. The inversion of courage turns out to be violence, and the inversion of wisdom, the virtue of the intellect, turns out to be fraud. Now, it's sort of interesting also to think about this in terms of the fourth important classical virtue, which is justice. Plato tells us a long time before Dante that if you have the other three, justice is going to be the well regulated version, the well regulated association of those three other virtues. Therefore, in the lack of all of those virtues is the unjust city that Dante is creating in this inversion, in this funnel that Bill talks about, and as Bill says, "The deeper the journey, the more serious the sin that he encounters there."

Cook: Another way we could talk about the progression, if you will, of sins is to suggest that what Dante's concerned about is not what we would think of as a criminal justice system, which thing on earth deserves the most years in prison; it's not that kind of system at all. Dante asks a fundamental question: What does it mean to be human? How does being human make us different than the other things that God created? One answer, again, goes back far before Dante, is humans have intellect, the faculty of knowing, and will, the faculty of choosing. As we're going to see, the sinners toward the top of hell are going to be those who essentially ignore those specifically human qualities, and the further we go down—the more we're going to see the conscious perversion of the human faculties of intellect and will.

Herzman: Now, who is it that we're going to see when we get down there? We've already given some pretty substantial clues in that direction. We've suggested, for example, that Dante the poet doesn't really make a distinction between real people and fictional people. We'll see people that really did exist; we'll also see people who are characters in works of literature, in mythology, and so on. We'll see figures who are from history, and we will also see figures, as we explained in some detail, who are "local." That is to say, who would have, perhaps, faded into oblivion were it not for the fact that Dante kind of keeps them alive for us in the poem. So, one of the things to keep in mind in the poem itself is this balance between concerns that are universal and concerns that are local. Going back and forth between these two is one of the chief things we ought to be looking for, and one of the things that makes this such a fascinating journey. So, there's this tremendous variety in when they lived and what kind of people they are.

What is it that all of these sinners have in common? Well, again, we go back to the definition. They're there because they are unrepentant, and because they are unrepentant they have this overwhelming compulsion, really, it's who they are, they have this overwhelming compulsion to justify what they've done to put the blame for the very actions that got them there somewhere else, and they do this in all kinds of interesting and subtle ways. One of our jobs, along with the job of Dante the pilgrim, is to try and unpack the kind of justifications that these sinners give for the deeds that they did back on earth and have got them where they are today.

Cook: If you find yourself scratching your head over one of these convincing speeches given by one of the sinners, and you say, "Really, am I supposed to buy this?" One of the things that should give you comfort is that Dante the pilgrim, the character that Dante the poet creates, is going to mess up a lot. He's going to misunderstand a lot. He's going to respond wrongly a lot. It's going to take a while for him to get oriented, and even as he begins to understand things, he will have lapses, so you should not be discouraged if, in fact, you say "Boy, I'm convinced this sinner really seemed like he or she shouldn't be there." We hope to guide you through some of that and help you get over some of those bumps, but it's important for you to have some of those bumps. It's important to have the experience that Dante the pilgrim has. It's a tough job decoding some very clever, very smart people we're going to meet in hell.

Herzman: Another way to take a look at what Bill has just said, one of the issues that Dante the poet has to deal with is that ultimately, if sin is destructive, and if it's destructive of those who commit it above all, after all they're here now and suffering for it, then why is it such a popular game? That is, why is it that so many people fall victim, if you will, to these sins? Well, one of the things that the poet needs to do is not only talk about the ultimate destructiveness of this sin, but also the kind of surface veneer of attractiveness that cause them to sort of think that it's really going to be fun. That veneer of attractiveness, especially at the beginning of hell, is also going to be there in the sinners' attempt to justify themselves, if you combine that with the fact that they have lost a kind of self-knowledge. We're told by Virgil after they actually get into the gates of hell that you have to be careful because here are the people who have lost the "good of intellect," and what that really turns out to be, what it means to lose the good of intellect, is the subject of the whole Inferno, but I think part of what it means is that they are able to tell a good story, but only within certain very narrow terms. They are people who see trees but don't see anything at all of the forest. So, when we go through hell, these are some of the things we ought to keep in mind, or better yet, these are things that we forget only at our peril. Our tendency, as Bill points out, is going to be—along with Dante the pilgrim—to sympathize with the sinners there, but we need to remind ourselves that the pilgrim that we see is somebody who wakes up in a dark wood of error, in a dark wood, and with that as a kind of introduction, we can turn to the text itself.

Cook: Dante's *Divine Comedy*, Inferno, Canto 1, line one.

> Midway along the journey of our life
> > I woke to find myself in a dark wood,
> > for I had wandered off from the straight path.
>
> How hard it is to tell what it was like,
> > the wood of wilderness, savage and stubborn
> > (the thought of it brings back all my old fears),

a bitter place! Death could scarce be bitterer.

> But if I would show the good that came of it
> I must talk about things other than the good.

How I enter there I cannot truly say,
> I had become so sleepy at the moment
> When I first strayed, leaving the path of truth;

Herzman: So, he is in a dark wood. It's pretty clear that he's very disoriented. He can't tell us what it was like, really, and he can't tell us how he got there. I guess the easiest explanation for that would be if he could, he'd know how to get out. If he could, it really wouldn't be this condition of disorientation. But it's also interesting to think about all of the different ways in which you can look at what the pilgrim is telling us about himself. Is this primarily about a kind of moral failure on his part? Is this primarily what we would consider a kind of mid-life crisis? After all, as we have already seen, this is exactly his mid-life, seems like as good a time as any to have a mid-life crisis. Is it some combination of that? Is it other things? Well, again, it's left somewhat vague, but I think what the poet is trying to say is that's part of the problem, that there's really no precise way, or more precise way, to define this terrible sense that he has of not knowing where he is, of where he's going, or even maybe where he's coming from.

Cook: To me, one modern author who helps to focus in on the condition of Dante the pilgrim is Hannah Arendt, the 20th century philosopher. She talks about, with regard to elements of the Holocaust, the banality of evil, and I think in some ways that's what Dante is expressing. It's not that he's just done some terrible thing and he wakes up and says, "Gosh, you shouldn't have done that." Instead, at some moment, he sort of looks at himself and his own story and says, "This isn't who I set out to be. This isn't what I meant to do. This isn't matching up very well with some of the things I wanted to do and some of the things I claim to be in favor of, some of the things I value. How did that happen?" It didn't happen in one great big leap, but presumably it happened in increments, and I think anybody, perhaps more our age than our students, but anybody can identify with that notion that every now and then you just say, "How did I get here? How did I end up defending this? How did I end up acting this way? This isn't, I think, who I am. This isn't what

I set out to be." I think that sense of being disoriented here is very much a part of that notion of the banality of evil.

Herzman: Of course, if the question is, number one, how did I get here, question number two is how do I get out? It seems like he has an easy answer to that question in the lines that immediately follow. He looks up, sees the sun.

> I raised my head and saw the hilltop shawled
> > in morning rays of light sent from the planet
> > that leads men straight ahead on every road.
>
> And then only did terror start subsiding
> > in my heart's lake, which rose to heights of fear
> > that night I spent in deepest desperation.

So, he talks about trying to kind of—he sees the sun and now he is going to try to climb to it.

> I rested my tired body there awhile
> > and then began to climb the barren slope
> > (I dragged my stronger foot and limped along).

Just as he's about to make the climb he's interrupted.

Cook: In fact, as he continues, he's interrupted three times by three different animals—a leopard, a lion, and a wolf, which by the way, in the Italian all begin with the letter "L." There's a beautiful sound to those three animals in Italian. What he discovers is that he simply can't get to the light on his own; these beasts will keep him from doing it. Dante scholars have argued around the periphery of what these stand for, but they all agree, virtually, that they stand for sin in general, and the three categories of sin that Ron's already described—incontinence, violence, and fraud. So, here's somebody who is in this sort of moral and spiritual disorientation, who says, "I think I can handle this on my own," and he turns out to be wrong.

Herzman: So, it would be a very short poem—instead of the 14,000 lines we have, you'd have like 32—if he sees the beasts and then he sort of goes back, back, as he says, to where the sun is mute. But, what happens is that somebody comes to rescue him. The second part of this first canto consists of Dante's meeting with the poet Virgil. The introduction of Dante to Virgil, the kind of surprise, the shock, of Dante meeting Virgil, and then the beginning of the process whereby he's going to get out of this mess when Virgil basically tells Dante that he has been sent; he is part of a heaven-sent mission to help Dante get out of this mess. Now, there's an awful lot to say about this, but let's start with the fact that it means that Dante's "salvation," Dante's ability to rescue himself here, doesn't come from within himself, it comes from help that he receives from the outside.

Cook: We would probably in theological terminology call this grace. That is to say that it is something free and undeserved, and toward the end of Canto 1, and in Canto 2, Virgil explains this process, beginning with the Virgin Mary, through Saint Lucy, and on to a woman named Beatrice, whom we've talked about before, and Beatrice actually sort of breaks the rules, as Virgil explains, comes down into limbo, the upper part of hell, where Virgil lives eternally, and says, "Virgil, I've got a job for you. I want you to go get this guy who is lost in a dark wood, and I want you to take him on a journey through the entire afterlife." Virgil doesn't take him all the way there, Virgil takes him about two-thirds of the way. "I'll meet you later on, and I'll take over at a certain point, but he's got to go through this journey. He's so messed up, things are so bad, that some of the normal ways you might try to correct people simply won't work. He's too far gone for sort of the normal remedies. He really needs this extraordinary journey."

Herzman: Yes, notice that it also is sort of interesting when Dante and Virgil meet here, that if you have Virgil as the one who is going to take him out of this, Dante himself says "This is really cool because you're the poet that I learned so much of my own writing style from. You're an appropriate guide." But, the fact is, Virgil is there to help Dante because others have come to Virgil and made him an offer he couldn't really refuse. So, we have Dante and Virgil hooked up, and they'll stay that way for 68 more cantos, but it's also interesting that Virgil's job is not yet done in terms of saying, "All right, it's a done deal, sign on the dotted line," because Dante seems to be quite reluctant to take the journey even after Virgil says, "I'm here to help you out" because, of course, he says, "You've got to go another way. See, you wanted to climb up, can't do that. The way to salvation for you, before you can even start thinking about going up, is to go down first." You've got to get down into the pit before you can rise. Well, in theory that sounds like a good idea, but the more Dante begins to think about it, the more he gets cold feet, gets a little bit terrified, and tries to back out. So, Virgil's job is ultimately to accompany Dante, but before he does that he has to kind of convince him to do it. Beginning at the second canto there's this wonderful stuff going on where Dante attempts to sort of weenie out of the deal, and Virgil convinces him that he has to go and do it.

Cook: Again, that arm-twisting takes a while, but finally Dante does go, and at the beginning of Canto 3 we actually enter hell. There's a formal gate, sort of looks like one of those Roman arches that survives in downtown Rome and other places, and the inscription on the gate contains the single most important line, or at least the most famous line, of the *Commedia*. It's worthwhile looking at that inscription which is at the beginning of Inferno 3.

> I am the way into the doleful city,
>> I am the way into eternal grief,
>> I am the way to a forsaken race.
>
> Justice it was that moved my great creator;
>> Divine omnipotence created me,
>> And highest wisdom joined with primal love.
>
> Before me nothing but eternal things
>> Were made, and I shall last eternally.
>> Abandon every hope, all you who enter.

Herzman: Now, of course, the thing that's most interesting about it from our point of view is that Dante is coming with Virgil as a kind of temporary visitor, not a permanent inhabitant, and so that last bit of advice, abandon all hope, doesn't really apply to him in that he has every expectation and promise of getting out. But, it must be a pretty scary experience for the pilgrim to embark upon the journey and that's what he sees as he begins. So, there's a sense in which he's going to have to really if not abandon hope, at least abandon his fear, in a very big-time way in order to kind of even begin to undertake what's going to happen once he's though the gates, where all of a sudden the action really begins to speed up and things begin to happen to the pilgrim, or at least he sees things all around him happening, at a pretty breakneck pace.

Cook: It's interesting that Dante's first response to that passage through the gate and to those nine lines that are inscribed on the gate is, "…these words I see are cruel." This is a sign for us that we don't necessarily have to understand Dante the pilgrim as our best guide right now because, in fact, the arch itself says this is a place of justice, and in some sense, with Dante saying these words are cruel, he seems not to accept that principle, certainly not accept it in its entirety. That's a sign to us that we need to remember that he's just left the dark wood. He's got an awful lot of learning to do. We do not accept the pilgrim's analysis of things at face value.

Herzman: Now, he's there, he's in hell, let the game begin, except that the first place is kind of an interesting anteroom or vestibule to hell, where a very unusual group is being punished. They haven't committed any specific sin, but they haven't done anything good either. In fact, they haven't done much of anything. In this anteroom what we find are the folks that have refused to take a stand on anything when they were still alive. They are the first inhabitants of the afterlife that Dante meets, and, essentially, we have to figure out what to do with these folks. What does it mean to have all of these people running around who have not taken any stand, made any decision, done anything at all back in their own life?

Cook: These neutrals are, in fact, important folks for us to meet up with because, I think, they sort of bring experience that we understand, but ultimately when we don't take a stand on anything, we simply say, "Gee, I'm not going to talk about that. I'll keep my opinions to myself," or "I'm not going to follow that cause or this cause," what we're essentially saying is I care more about me than I do about anything else. If I take a stand, somebody's going to dislike me. If I take a stand, I might be on the losing side, and that's not good for me. Therefore, while we might think about neutrality as a kind of Olympian view of judging everything carefully and rationally, Dante's not opposed to judging everything rationally, mind you, but what Dante fears are those who ultimately will not take stands, or those who really stand only for themselves, and therefore part of their punishment is Dante never names any of them. They are condemned to a kind of anonymity in hell. That way of looking at this very first set of "sinners" is a clue to the way we're going to see group after group of sinners punished, that what they chose in some real way is what they get, with what Ron said earlier, that nice veneer that sometimes makes sin attractive to us, taken away.

Herzman: Of course, also, this is another way for the poet to let us know that refusing to choose really is a choice. That the sense that you're not choosing is a kind of illusion, a kind of scam that you're playing, possibly on yourself, but a scam definitely because not taking a stand, not making a choice, is going to have consequences, and another one of the things that we pick up here is that the poem is very concerned with showing the sin not only in terms of what it is in itself, what it does to the sinner, but what other consequences exist. How doing things, or in this case not doing things, really sets out a kind of pattern of reverberation where a lot of people are implicated in what is done, and that, too, is present as one of the kind of preliminary lessons that we learn about this section of hell.

Cook: At the end of Canto 3 we go down to the next step, and that is the first of these formal nine circles, and yet it's very different from the eight circles that we will subsequently pass through, because here the punishment is not so obvious. There are no tortures, no shrieks, no screams, and it sort of sounds like—from the description—it's a nice place. It's a place that's called "limbo," and it is here that Dante meets up with folks we usually call the "virtuous pagans," and also very importantly, one of the permanent residents here is, in fact, the guy that is temporarily released to become Dante's guide—this is to say, this is Virgil's dwelling in the afterlife.

Herzman: Now, this—sometimes I like to think of the vestibule, the cantos that we've just seen, as hell with an asterisk, and then Canto 4, circle one here, as hell with a double asterisk because, as Bill suggests, one of the things that separates this from all of the other places that we're going to see is that there really is no punishment as such, but it's also interesting to think about this as different from other places in hell in that there is a very interesting thing that takes place a long time ago that affects the people who used to be there and who aren't there any longer. In other words, this is the only place in hell where it was not eternal, where there was a kind of holding pattern for folks who were there for a while and who are not there now, and who have, in fact, gone up to heaven. So, it is sort of like there are two classes of people here, those virtuous pagans who look like they are going to spend eternity here, and the folks who used to be here but aren't any more.

Cook: There is a story that really isn't biblical but nevertheless that comes out of some very early Christian teaching that says when Christ died on the cross, he went down into hell and released the faithful Jews' it's called the "Harrowing of Hell," and it is often depicted in medieval art with Christ coming down there, knocking down the door, trampling on a demon, and holding onto the hands of Adam and Eve, with other faithful Jews lined up behind. In fact,

Dante names a whole crowd of faithful Jews who were let out. So, this great exception to the rule of abandon all hope you who enter here is, in fact, told. After all, Virgil died in 19 B.C., and as he said, "I was a fairly recent resident here when that happened."

Herzman: So, the question is, what particular importance does that have to this story as it relates to Dante's own journey? One way to take a look at it is that the pattern of Christ coming down into hell and then rising up again really is the pattern of Dante's own journey. In other words, Dante is doing precisely what—in this story—Christ did while he was in the tomb. He comes down; he leads others out. Well, Dante, of course, is not going to lead anybody else out except in a kind of metaphorical way when you can think about the poem itself as Dante taking souls out of hell, taking them out of tendencies toward sin that they might have had. But, again, it shows you that there is a kind of exception to the rule in this particular circle that we're not going to see in any other place in hell, but it's a good way to have us think about the fact that Dante the poet builds systems and then shows us exceptions to the systems that he builds. It's one of the patterns that we'll see in other parts of the *Commedia* as well.

Cook: Dante has exciting experiences here in limbo, where the punishment, we're told, really is that those who are here live on in desire, desire for the highest things, which, of course, in the Christian scheme is God, but live on without hope, nevertheless, there are not screams and tortures, and Dante meets up and has a sort of pleasant conversation with a number of poets, including Homer, and then Dante is sort of introduced around to a whole array of important classical figures, some of the ones you would most expect would be here—Plato, Aristotle, Socrates, Cicero, Julius Caesar, some less famous figures as well, but also, interestingly enough, because we tend to think about these as folks who after all died before Jesus came and therefore didn't have any knowledge, if they weren't Jews, even of the coming of Jesus. But there are also three medieval Muslim figures here, which again reminds us that this scheme is more complex than it might seem. It's not easy to reduce anything Dante does to a one-liner.

Herzman: What makes things even more complicated is that we're going to see in other parts of the *Commedia* pagans as well. So, this is the first of Dante's dealing with the very, very difficult problem of salvation for non-believers.

Lecture Six
The Never-Ending Storm

Scope:

In this lecture, we examine the nature of incontinence—subjecting reason to desire—by examining lust, the sin explored in Inferno 5. Here, the pilgrim meets many figures but has a sustained encounter with one of them, Francesca da Rimini. Because this is the first sustained encounter that Dante has with a figure of the afterlife, it is a particularly important scene for understanding the nature of hell and the essence of all the sins encountered there. Francesca tells Dante the story of how she was drawn into an illicit relationship with her silent lover Paolo, her husband's brother. Like all sinners in the Inferno, Francesca puts the blame elsewhere. The pilgrim, who is himself more than a little inclined toward this sin, feels sorry for Francesca. But Dante the writer gives the reader a great many important clues to suggest that this is not the proper response to her narrative.

Outline

I. If Dante is journeying toward God, why does he need to go to hell?

    A. He needs to descend in order to ascend.

    B. He needs to learn the nature of sin from the unrepentant.

    C. He needs to learn how to overcome these same tendencies in himself.

    D. The sinners whom he spends the most time with are those who have the most to say to him personally and in terms of his own moral development.

    E. These sinners help teach the reader about Dante.

    F. The sinners' plights and punishments are not arbitrarily imposed; on the contrary, they are freely self-chosen.

II. In Canto 5, the circle of the lustful, we have the first sustained encounter between Dante and an unrepentant sinner.

    A. We are now in hell "without an asterisk."

    B. This encounter tells us about the nature of the sin.

C. It also tells us something about the "rules" for hell more generally and about the nature of all sins.

D. Finally, the encounter tells us about the pilgrim's own situation.

III. The sin of lust is described through the very geography of the region.

    A. Sinners are whirled about in a never-ending storm.

    B. This storm corresponds to the nature of lust, defined with the other sins of incontinence as submitting reason to desire.

IV. The sin is also described by the list of famous inhabitants of this circle.

    A. Dido helps us learn about the sin. Dante the poet blames her in a way that rewrites Virgil's Dido.

    B. Dido remains an important presence in the poem.

V. In a lengthy encounter, Dante meets Francesca da Rimini, a "front-page news item" from his own time.

    A. Her description of her adulterous affair is one of the famous dramatic moments of the poem.

    B. She explains her story to Dante while Paolo, her lover, remains silently at her side.

    C. She blames love and a book—the courtly tale of Lancelot and Guenivere's adultery—for her fate.

        1. Like all sinners, she shifts the blame from herself.

        2. Like all sinners, she embodies massive self-centeredness.

    D. Dante is drawn in by her story and feels sorry for her.

    E. Yet the text provides many clues to suggest that her choice was deliberately made.

    F. Her story ends with an echo of Augustine's conversion in the *Confessions.*

        1. That allusion to Augustine's famous *tolle lege* allows the poet to undercut her position.

        2. It also shows that the canto is concerned with proper ways of reading a text.

        3. This, too, is an important lesson for the pilgrim to learn.

Readings:

Augustine, *The Confessions*, Book 8.

Dante, *Inferno*, Canto 5.

Questions to Consider:

1. Why does Dante the pilgrim feel such sympathy for Francesca and Paolo?

2. How does the punishment fit the crime, or better, how is the sin embodied in the punishment of the lustful?

3. Why is lust regarded as the least serious sin in hell?

Lecture Six—Transcript
The Never-Ending Storm

Cook: In the previous lecture, we spent at least a little bit of time in Cantos 1, 2, 3, and 4. However, we are not going to mention, at least in any detail, most of the cantos from here on. That is to say what we're going to be doing is looking at representative cantos in each of the major parts of hell, and then we'll talk about purgatory and heaven later on, but in doing this, spending more time analyzing less, what we want to do is be able to provide you with some tools so you will be better readers on your own of the other parts. We want to make sure that you have a chance to explore Dante not just with us, but also on your own, and so as we enter into the second circle, one of four circles in the category of sin called incontinence, we're first going to meet up with those who are called "the lustful," and in doing so we are going to have one of the most dramatic encounters of the entire *Commedia*—one that has been talked about, written about, and a lot of music has been composed about, and that is the meeting between Dante and Francesca and Paulo, but first, something about how we enter into this particular section of the Inferno.

Herzman: It's sort of interesting that here when we're in hell without any asterisks whatsoever, the first thing that we see is it's got a judge, and the judge is there to give people their appropriate place in the afterlife, the monster, the classical monster—Minos—that Dante takes and he puts here; he sort of rings his tail around himself the number of times he wants to send this sinner down, so six rings you go down to the sixth circle, and he serves as the guardian of hell in general. We know that we are in it big-time after we get there, but it's sort if interesting to see what we get to when we pass by Minos and are now ready to have this, as Bill said, sustained encounter with the lustful. What we get is a very interesting sort of geography presented to us. We've already mentioned the fact that we're likely to have a physical geography, which is at the same time a kind of moral geography. It's sort of nifty to see the way that works in what you get as the sort of placement of the lustful because geography is very much implicated in the punishment for the sin here.

Cook: We discover that the sinners are sort of blowing around in an infernal storm, to use Dante's phrase in line 31 in Canto 5. They are sort of blowing around and what's interesting is that for every puff and gust of wind it sort of bumps them up and down and around. They're totally out of control. Wherever any air current, if you will, takes them, that is where they will go. In fact, Dante likens them to birds we still see in Italy who lay their wings out in the evening, so therefore as you look at them it looks like they are nice and smooth and floating, but they'll in fact constantly be bumping because, of course, they will be taken up and down by every single little bitty air pocket.

Herzman: So, this is one of the best places, pretty close to the beginning, to see the way in which the punishment is a reflection of the sin. The words that Bill used that I think are the ones that kind of should key our attention: "out of control," because, of course, it is the nature of the sin itself to be out of control, but that's sort of a good definition, or at least as good a modern definition of lust that you might want to find, and so you get this very interesting picture, literally, of sinners in the afterlife getting what they wanted back on earth, and that's a very important part of the system of Dante's hell—in the afterlife, you get what you want. They wanted to be out of control, and that's what they get. Notice the language:

> and as the wings of starlings in the winter
>> bear them along in wide-spread crowded flocks,
>> so does that wind propel the evil spirits.

> Now here, then there, and up and down, it drives them
>> with never any hope to comfort them—
>> hope not of rest but even of suffering less.

So, it's sort of this flock of birds who turn out not to be birds at all, but souls buffeted by the wind; they are the lustful, and there's a whole mess of them there, and the technique here the poet uses is very interesting and very instructive of the way he works throughout. You'll see a lot of sinners there identified; then, we concentrate on just a couple of them. Then, we concentrate even more on one sinner, as Bill said, the famous Francesca da Rimini, whose story Dante gets to hear in great detail. So, we go from geography to sort of the group picture, and then from a group picture to a sort of small group photo, and then from a small group photo to the dramatic dialogue, the dramatic interchange between Dante and an inhabitant of the afterlife, and since this is the first sustained encounter, between Dante and a permanent inhabitant of the afterlife, for that reason too it's worth our attention because it tells us not only about the nature of this particular sin, it also tells us a whole lot about how to read the Inferno, what to look for, what the kind of characteristic ploys of the sinners are, and so on down a very long list.

Cook: This introduction around that Dante receives really is a pretty interesting cast of characters. For example, we find Cleopatra—that might not be such a surprise, we find the great hero Achilles, one of the most important figures we find, this would be in line 61,

> The next is she who killed herself for love
> and broke faith with the ashes of Sichaeus;

You may recall this is a person we've already mentioned a couple times. It's a way of showing how the introductory material is going to make reading the Inferno a little bit more meaningful, because we talked about her, she is Dido, as a character in the *Aeneid*, in fact sort of the dominant character along with Aeneas, in Book IV, and then we talked about her again when we went to the *Confessions* of Saint Augustine and talked about how Augustine tells of reading the story in the *Aeneid* of Dido. Now, we know where Dido's own place is in the afterlife, and Dante, although he will not converse with Dido, mentions her a couple of times, and therefore really is reminding us that we need to cash in on what we know about the whole catalog of stories and interpretations of Dido in order fully to understand what he is doing here.

Herzman: In fact, Dido is one of the characters in this particular canto who sort of provides us with a kind of signature to it. It's in a way, it becomes of course Francesca's canto, but in a way it's Dido's canto as well because when Dante wants to find this one particular pair of sinners to talk to, notice what he says,

> I raised my voice to them, 'Oh wearied souls,
> come speak with us if it is not forbidden.'

> As doves, called by desire to return
> to their sweet nest with wings raised high and poised,
> float downward through the air, guided by will,

> so these two left the flock where Dido is

In other words, this is sort of Dido's flock in a very real way. But in any case, what happens is that you have these two sinners leave the flock, come to Dante, and we have, then, the first sustained encounter between the pilgrim and a figure of the afterlife, and it's interesting that it is the figure that begins speaking first. She speaks to Dante before Dante speaks to her:

Cook:

> 'O living creature, gracious and so kind,
>> who makes your way here through this dingy air
>> to visit us, who stained the world with blood,'

And so on. What an odd way to begin. "Oh living creature," not "Hey fella" or anything else, but in fact the Italian word is *animal*. We, of course, use it to mean mammals and all that sort of stuff; the word literally means "Oh animated thing," "Oh living thing," thing with an *anima*, a soul. Why would she refer to him by this very generic word rather than recognize his humanity? Well, if we think about the sin of incontinence, the sin of incontinence is the sin of ignoring—sort of rejecting, putting aside, not using—the specifically human gifts of intellect and will. That's what she's done, that's why she's here, and therefore just as it's gone in her, she does not recognize Dante's humanity, she does not recognize what it is that makes Dante specifically a human being. So, from the very first words that Francesca speaks, she's telling us much more than she thinks she's telling us about herself, and that will remain true as long as she speaks in Inferno 5.

Herzman: In fact, in that very same line, she turns to Dante and says, "gracious and so kind." Well, what she's saying to Dante is you have done me a really special favor of coming down to hell to pay a little social call. Well, we have to remember, we have to remind ourselves, again, it's a really good example of what Bill said about Francesca's point of view not being ours. The fact is Dante's not there to pay a social call to Francesca; he's there because this is a last-ditch final attempt to do something that will get him out of this deep, deep spiritual malaise. This is what you do when nothing else is going to work. This is a kind of shock treatment for the soul that Dante is getting, and yet she looks upon it as though this is a kind of out of the way and fairly extravagant social call. You've come all the way to see me—what that indicates pretty clearly is that, like every other soul that we encounter in the Inferno, Francesca fully and completely believes that she is the exact center of the universe, and everything is seen in relation to that centrality. Notice, for example, she also says, "if we could claim as friend the King of Kings," if it happened that we were on speaking terms with God, then we would ask "him that he grant you peace." We're not, as though once again this is some sort of minor social tiff that they're having that will be fixed up sooner or later, but, again, that sense of total disregard for where she is, a kind of oblivion to what it means to be down there and seeing things merely in terms of a set of social relations. Notice also that she is speaking—this would be medieval language as much as modern—with great courtesy and elegance, as though courtesy and elegance were really all you need to get on in life, and, indeed, once she tells her story, or as she continues to tell her story, that courtesy and that elegance is sort of the dominant picture that we get as she continues.

Cook: Let's take a look at the way she begins to explain the story of her life, specifically the story of the end of her life.

> 'Love, quick to kindle in the gentle heart,
>> seized this one (Paolo next to her) for the beauty of my body,
>> torn from me, (How it happens still offends me!)
>
> Love, that excuses no one loved from loving,
>> seized me so strongly with delight in him
>> that, as you see, he never leaves my side.
>
> Love led us straight to sudden death together.'

Notice what she's doing here. We were teaching this story once inside a prison, and we were reading that passage. One of the inmates put up his hand and said, "That's me. That's why I'm here." "That is to say," he went on to explain to us, "I used to do that all the time. I'd do something wrong and I'd find something else to blame for it. I would never look at myself as the cause of the problem." Listen to Francesca's language again, "Love seized me, love seized me, love led us." She creates this personification of love, a certain kind of love, of course, and then she says love made me do it. I had no choice. I had no control over my own self; this is something love forced me, forced us, primarily me, forced us to do.

Herzman: Notice that in doing that, in putting the blame on love, she's making love sound like a kind of independent being, another kind of *animal* if you will, another kind of being with a soul, and in personifying love, it is therefore able to shift the blame, as though love were there with an AK-47 saying, "You will do what I tell you." In so doing, as Bill says, she's the first to sort of shift the blame

©2001 The Teaching Company

somewhere else, but what she's also doing is using a kind of language that poets in Dante's own time used in their own love poetry, and, indeed, not all that different from the language of Dante's own earlier love poetry. So, Francesca sort of sounds like a character from a Harlequin Romance, if we're using modern categories, but if we're using somewhat older categories, she sounds a little bit like characters you might read about in the poetry of Dante's youth. I think this is extremely important because when Dante responds to her, one of the things that he does is respond with an enormous amount of pity. It's almost as though Francesca's story moves him so deeply because it's a story if not actually about himself, about the kind of stuff that he also was used to writing.

So, there's something very personal here, and it speaks toward the fact that when Dante has long conversations with sinners, it's almost always because those sinners have something special to tell him. In other words, it's almost as though what he is seeing in these sinners are kind of mirrors of aspect or part of his own life. In a sense, what he has to do is learn from these sinners how to overcome those same tendencies in his own life, but, of course, right now at the beginning, hardly removed at all from the dark wood of error, his tendency rather is to sympathize with them instead of listening and saying, "My goodness, what a crock is this," he is enormously affected and moved by it, so affected and so moved that, in fact, he wants to hear a whole lot more about what's going on.

> 'Alas,' (again, Dante is the one who is speaking)
> 'all those sweet thoughts, and oh, how much desiring
> brought you two down into this agony.'

He's hooked, okay? If this is a Harlequin Romance, maybe it is also a kind of soap opera, and he can't wait to get to the next episode. So, he asks Francesca, tell me more about this; tell me how it happened in really excruciating detail.

Cook: As it turns out—both up to now, and in the story that she's about to tell more elaborately—she leaves out some things. Now, obviously, whenever we tell a story we make certain decisions about what we say, but we've got Francesca with this guy Paolo in an area where the lustful are being punished. Here's a detail she leaves out: She's married, but not to Paolo. That's fairly important. Number two, Paolo is the brother of her husband. That is to say, she's there with her brother-in-law in this sort of barren embrace as they're being whirled around. Those are sort of important facts to know. It sort of helps us to understand who Francesca is. She leaves them out, and we have them in a translation like this because they're in the notes. That's why looking at notes, at least occasionally, is a useful thing to do because you cannot trust these sinners to tell you the whole story. They tell you what they want you to hear because they think in some way it will justify their position.

Herzman: Of course, in this particular case, this was a kind of well known—our phrase would be tabloid story—from a little bit before Dante's time. He's aware of who she is in the middle of this story. This was, if not "front-page news," back-page news on whatever the Italian equivalent of the *National Enquirer* would be, and, in fact, the other detail is that they were caught in the act by her husband, her lover's brother, who killed them on the spot, and that's sort of what gets them to where they are here. So, in leaving all of that out, she's not only leaving out stuff that Dante's audience would have been well aware of, but leaving out all of the things that might ask us to take a moral stance here. I mean, jeepers, what about doing it with your husband's brother? But, again, her language is simply it was love, love made us do it, and then, as she gets even more specific, when Dante says,

> 'how…did love enable [sic allow] you
> to recognize your dubious desires?'

How did this stuff start?" Her story is even more ingenious in some ways because of the really wonderful way in which she's able to put off the blame yet once again.

Cook:

> 'One day we read, to pass the time away,
>   of Lancelot, of how he fell in love;
>   we were alone, innocent of suspicion.'

Okay, there are a lot of things here we need to think about. First of all, she and her brother-in-law were alone, and they had a book, a very famous story, the story of Lancelot, the story of the round table. We need to ask ourselves for a minute what is the basic lesson, or at least a basic lesson, of that whole story? I suppose one way to summarize it is when one of your knights is having an affair with your wife, the king's wife is having an affair with a knight, when that's happening, it's sort of hard to have the round table, sort of hard to work out how you keep Camelot, and so, if you will, there are very important moral lessons to be learned in that story, despite the fact the story has a lot of romance and intrigue and excitement in it. How would you find that moral lesson? Or, to put it another way, as a question, would you find it if you read the book simply to pass the time away?

Herzman: One of the ways that we update it is to sort of suggest that the modern equivalent would be to say, "Let's jump on the waterbed and put maybe an R to X-rated, video in the VCR, and see, well, if anything is going to happen, but it's really all innocent," because, in other words, when she says "to pass the time away," in Italian the phrase is even more pointed, the phrase is *per diletto*, which, when I do my translation of the *Commedia* I'm going to translate as "one day we read for kicks." It's kind of the equivalent of (in my youth) when censorship laws were a lot stronger than they are now, and the class was passing around the secret version of *Lady Chatterley's Lover*. You'd already know what the good passages were because they were all dog-eared. You wouldn't have to read the book; you could just go to the smut. Well, essentially, what she seems to be doing is reading it not for the moral, but reading it as a kind of how-to manual. She's reading it, in other words, for instruction. As she tells us immediately after, she's reading in the book, and then time and again—well, first of all, that wonderful line, "We were alone, innocent of suspicion." I think it's a valid question to ask whether you can be reading this sort of book alone with your husband's brother and be innocent of suspicion, but even if you were willing to give her the benefit of the doubt here, which I think most certainly we don't want to do, take a look at what she says immediately afterwards:

> 'Time and again our eyes were brought together
>   by the book we read;...'

Well, at this point are we still to say they were without any kind of suspicion?

> '...our faces flushed and paled.
> To the moment of one line alone we yielded:
>
> it was when we read about those longed-for lips'
>   now being kissed by such a famous lover,'

Well, again, she doesn't necessarily want us to get this out of what she's saying, but it's hard not to. They're using it as a kind of how-to manual. They look and see what they're doing in the book, we imitate it ourselves, and, again, notice that she's saying that it was the book that brought us together to that, and she even says that in even more explicit detail as the text goes on.

Cook: She goes on to say,

> 'then kissed my mouth, and trembled as he did.
> Our Galehot was that book and he who wrote it.'

Well, Galehot was, of course, a character in the Lancelot story, the go-between between Guinevere and Lancelot. In fact, in some terms the term "Galehot" can mean a kind of pimp, the one that makes all the arrangements, a procurer, if you will. So, here she says it's the book that did it. She's already said love did it, love made us do this, love seized us, love led us, and whatever; now, it's the book that did it, it's the book's fault. Well, there's plenty of blame, and she's passing it all around, and it seems to belong everyplace but on Francesca, and it is very important to see that, that if you think about one of the ultimate consequences of saying love did it, or the book did it, it is I have no freedom of the will; I have no faculty of choosing; I'm simply being manipulated by these impersonal forces—whether it's love or whether it's a particular book—and it's very easy for Dante the pilgrim, for the reader, to buy into that. It's going to take a very careful reader to see how Francesca is speaking to us, and how we should respond to it.

Herzman: Notice that Francesca's position here is, as Bill said, I didn't really make a choice. This stuff kind of happened to me, the book made me do it just as love did. Well, in that sense, having kind of given over her freedom of the will, that's reflected in the punishment. We can now kind of go back and think about her being blown all around as somebody who has given up will and freedom, that it's kind of nifty, again, to see how the moral geography of the poem operates as part of the punishment. Notice also that when she's saying I really had no choice, love called, I answered, the book says hey, do it, I did it, she also is, in a way, reenacting that in the very story that she's telling to Dante here. What I mean by that is simply this, Dante says, "Hey, tell me a little bit more about how this all happened," and Francesca says,

> ...'There's really no greater pain
> than to remember, in our present grief,
> past happiness...'

But if this is your desire I'll certainly do it. In other words, Dante is asking her to do something that ultimately is going to cause her a great deal of pain, and she's willing to because she seems to be a girl who just can't say no, and what she did back on earth is now duplicated, replicated, in the position that she's in hell here. So, she responds to Dante's call and does something that is ultimately bringing her pain. Notice that that, too, is a very good definition of what Dante the poet means by sin, doing something that ultimately is destructive. Here, as in so many of the other examples that we see, the person who is most harmed by any particular sin, by every sin in hell, is the sinner primarily, others secondarily, and Francesca illustrates this in a particularly vivid way. She's not done yet.

Cook: The punch line, the last line she speaks, in fact, in the encounter with Dante, this is line 138, "That day we read no further." One passage, one kiss, put the book down. Well, the obvious question to ask is, "Why?" And, I think the answer is pretty obvious, because they went right into the old sackaroo together, and of course, while they were in the sack together her husband, Paolo's brother, comes home and kills them both. So, it's an interesting line that tells us what this story has really been leading to all along. We sort of knew it; she knows it, but at any rate she tries to tell it differently, but what's interesting is that line is virtually a quotation from a story, from the story of another person who was affected by lust—a fellow named Saint Augustine.

Herzman: As it turns out, we talked a little bit in a previous lecture about the importance in Book 8 in the *Confessions* where Augustine is converted. Augustine is converted by reading a book, and the book that he's reading is by Paul, Saint Paul. Francesca here, of course, her lover is Paul, Paolo is Paul in Italian, and in both cases what happens is that they take up a book and read it. Augustine is told by the voice of the child to take the book and read. He picks up Paul, Paul tells him to give up not only his lust in particular, but all manner of unseemly revelry, and he says at that moment, "That day I read no further, nor was there need." In other words, at that exact moment, Augustine was converted. His will turned from the self toward God. What Dante is doing is taking that passage, echoing it here to show

how in Francesca exactly the same thing happens but in exactly the opposite direction. As Augustine is turned from self to God, Francesca is turned from God to self, through Paolo, and what we see is that—as in Augustine—this is the moment when his will enters into the conversion when he chooses. This is Dante's wonderfully subtle way of saying that Francesca, too, despite all of her claims to the contrary, despite all of this stuff about saying love made me do it and the book made me do it, turns her will, makes a choice, and of course, here has to live with the consequences of that choice.

Now, it's interesting also if you take a look at that day we read the "no further" line in another way. Bill has given you all the reasons why they weren't reading any further, and, of course, they didn't read much further because they got to the sack, and then they got to the sack, and then they got killed. The husband comes in and catches them in the act, kills them right there on the spot. A little bit earlier, when Francesca was talking about how love did this and love did that, and love was so powerful and I couldn't help myself, the final punch line of that little speech in favor of love,

'Love led us straight to sudden death together.
Caïna awaits the one who quenched our lives.'

Caïna is one of the places that Dante has at the very, very bottom of hell for folks who are guilty of treachery, and what Francesca is saying is, that SOB that killed us is going to get his. Now, whether or not that's true we have no way of knowing, for all we know, her husband repented. Francesca I don't think has any special insight here, but the deal is Francesca's talking all this sweet talk about love, love, love it's so wonderful, and the last line, the punch line, is hate for the SOB that did it to me. Well, one way of taking a look at that is that's a pretty narrow way of thinking about love that the love that she's talking about actually turns out to be so narrowly focused that it's only about herself.

Cook: After Dante hears this story, he faints. Dante the pilgrim just collapses and faints; it's such a sad story. It grips him so that he just can't stand it. I think what we can say as our final take on this canto is, Dante, you've got a lot of learning left to do, it's only Canto 5, you've got a ways to go. We'll pick up the story shortly after this event happens.

Lecture Seven
Heretics

Scope:

Dante's Inferno deals with sins of wrong belief, as well as wrong action. In this lecture, we analyze Canto 10, where sinners are punished for heresy. According to Christian doctrine, heresy is the sin of wrong belief. But Dante's analysis goes much deeper than the textbook definition. In this circle are punished the Ghibelline leader Farinata and his Guelf tombmate Cavalcante. Dante links the sin of heresy with partisan politics. The pilgrim's encounter with these two sinners is especially dramatic, because it deals with two of his own major interests. With Farinata, he argues about politics and with Cavalcante, he discusses poetry. In both cases, we see that heresy, like partisan politics, can be seen as a division, a separation of things that should be whole. In this canto, we also see the first clear prediction of Dante's exile.

Outline

I.   In Canto 10, the sixth circle of hell, Dante finds the heretics.

    A. Hell deals with wrong belief, as well as wrong action.

    B. Heresy, one kind of wrong belief, is presented after the circles of incontinence and before violence.

    C. Heresy, being a uniquely "Christian" sin, fits somewhat uneasily into these categories, which are based on classical virtues.

II. In this canto, we learn about heresy indirectly through two major encounters with sinners.

    A. The first significant sinner Dante encounters here talks about politics.

    B. The second talks about poetry.

    C. Both of these are major concerns of the pilgrim.

    D. They also get at some of the major presuppositions of heresy.

III. Dante is accosted by Farinata, an important Ghibelline leader in the generation before Dante's birth, who recognizes Dante because of his Tuscan "mode of speech."

  A. Farinata the Ghibelline and Dante the Guelf aggressively go after each other, recreating in hell the bitterness of partisan politics in Florence.

  B. Farinata, an especially proud figure, taunts Dante about the superiority of his family and his ancestors (and, of course, himself).

  C. Dante rises to the bait and answers in kind.

IV. They are interrupted by Cavalcante, the father of one of Dante's fellow Florentine poets and his friend Guido Cavalcante.

  A. He baits Dante by talking about poetry and about how his son is better at it than Dante is.

  B. He seems to view coming to hell as a prize that Dante has won instead of his son.

  C. Once again, Dante rises to the bait.

V. When Cavalcante falls back into the tomb, Farinata resumes his discussion with the poet as though nothing had happened.

  A. Farinata predicts Dante's exile.

  B. He "justifies" his political actions in an entirely self-serving way.

  C. He answers Dante's questions about souls being able to see into the future.

VI. This discussion of politics and poetry gets to the nature of heresy on a deep level.

  A. Heresy separates what should be whole.

  B. This is true of politics and poetry, as well as doctrine.

  C. Both politics and poetry are concerned with proper and improper uses of language, which remains an important issue throughout this canto.

  D. Dante the pilgrim is very much in danger of these tendencies, whether or not he was ever a heretic in any formal sense.

Readings:

Erich Auerbach, *Mimesis: The Representation of Reality in Western Literature*, "Farinata and Cavalcante."

Dante, *Inferno*, Cantos 6–10.

Questions to Consider:

1. Why does Dante talk about politics and poetry in Inferno 10 when the sinners are being punished for the sin of heresy?

2. How do we see Dante the pilgrim participating in the sin of heresy along with the sinners?

3. Why are poetry and politics areas that often seem to bring out the worst in people?

Lecture Seven—Transcript
Heretics

Herzman: Francesca da Rimini, who we looked at extensively in the last lecture, can certainly be looked at as the poster child for the sin of lust, but I suppose we could also look at her as the poster child for the whole category of incontinence, the whole kind of general area. Lust certainly is the most interesting of the sins of incontinence, and also I think had a special place for Dante for what we already said, namely that this was something that he was himself implicated in, but also as Augustine tells us in the *Confessions,* this is a sin that we're all implicated in. So, kind of starting things off with lust makes a lot of sense in his scheme, but it's important for us to remember that depending on what the object is, the way in which you submit reason to desire, you can commit the sin in a number of other interesting varieties. So, after lust we get gluttony, which is incontinence, subjecting reason to desire as it relates to food and drink. After that, we have folks who are incontinent, who subject reason to desire with respect to money. We have the hoarders and the wasters. Then, after that, we have one more category, those who are incontinent with respect to their own emotions, people who are either angry or sullen, people who are flying off the handle all the time or are kind of enclosed down within themselves. So, in those cantos we move through the whole large area of incontinence, and then are sort of heading toward the second big category, that of violence, but not before making a very important and very interesting stop along the way at a place that doesn't quite fit into that scheme that we sketched out of incontinence, violence, and fraud.

Cook: That's a sin of heresy. This scheme of incontinence, violence, and fraud, in fact, Dante tells us, is derived from classical sources, and because of that there really is no place in this scheme for the sin of wrong belief, a specifically "Christian" sin, if you will. So, we come to this place where the heretics are punished, but we need to say a couple of things before we actually turn to the text.

First of all, we tend to think of our dictionary definition of heresy as some rejection of the formal teachings of the Church, and, indeed, Dante gives us suggestions that the people he meets here are indeed guilty of that. But what's interesting here and in several other places in Inferno, Dante does not talk about the sin in its literal form. We are not going to talk about theology and doctrine in this particular canto. We're going to talk about something very, very different, and therefore, as we look at the discussions that Dante has with two different sinners in this particular place, we want to ask ourselves what do these discussions of politics and poetry have to do with the sin of heresy? Why would that be a relevant topic of discussion, not just for Dante the pilgrim, where it's obvious because he was politician and poet, but why would it be a good conversation to have with people who are there being punished for heresy?

Herzman: Notice also that what Bill said is important in terms of these two concerns. We have politics—something that they talk about, poetry—something that they talk about, and each has a kind of separate character who deals with Dante on the way. So, in a way, dramatically, he's kind of a poet, he's kind of expanded the canvas a little bit. When you see the pilgrim encountering the sinners, he sees not one but two in this canto. So, it's sort of a complicated, carefully orchestrated thing. We see Dante walking along, and all of a sudden what happens here—

Cook:

> 'O Tuscan walking through our flaming city
>   alive, and speaking with such elegance,
>   be kind enough to stop here for a while.
>
> Your mode of speech identifies you clearly
>   as one whose birthplace is that noble city
>   with which in my time, perhaps, I was too harsh.'

Herzman: What we see is the pilgrim interrupted, encountered by the sinner rather than the other way around, by somebody who sort of grabs him and calls him a Tuscan, that is to say I know what area of Italy you're from by your mode of speech, as we would probably say your accent. What happens is that Dante is very confused, he turns around to Virgil as if to say, "What's up?" and Virgil says, "Turn around, that guy is Farinata. Pay attention to him and see what he has to tell you."

Cook: It's interesting that the punishment here is to be inside flaming tombs, and as Dante had begun to walk through there with Virgil, all he saw were the tombs with flames. Now this guy sort of rises up sort of waist high out of the tomb and speaks in this big, deep voice with a commanding presence. In fact, Dante's comment is he's "proclaiming his disdain for all this Hell." Then, Farinata begins to question Dante, wants to know a little bit more about him, more than he is just a Florentine. He asked, to use Dante's words, half-contemptuously, "And *who* would *your* ancestors be?"

Herzman: Now, that's a kind of curious question. Again, figure out the context, walking along, flaming tombs in hell, you see somebody, you recognize that person as a fellow citizen of your own part of the world, and the first thing you want to know, tell me about your ancestors. Say what? I mean, what does Farinata think is going on here, or what's he trying to get out of Dante, what's he doing? Dante, again, is put on the defensive. I think what's really interesting here is the way in which Farinata assumes control of the situation. We'll talk about the way he's sort of standing there, majestically. I like to think of him posing for the statue of himself, which he's hoping one of these days Florence is going to erect in his honor, sort of all puffed out and making sure that Dante is sort of backpedaling here when he does this wonderful gesture of lifting up his brows a little, as he puts it, and says,

> …'Bitter enemies of mine they were
> and of my ancestors and of my party;
> I had to scatter them, not once but twice.'

Now, what is going on there?

Cook: So, we have this situation where, you know, to put it real simply, here are two guys from the same hometown, a long way away from their hometown. We're a long way from Florence, and we might expect that a conversation between two Florentines would be about their Florentineness, if you will, what they have in common as citizens of the same country. But no, notice what this question is all about. First of all, is your family as good as mine, where the answer, by the way, inevitably will be no. Is the Alighieri family—that was Dante's family name—really as good? We know who this fellow is, Farinata, of the degli Uberti family. Then, secondly, because party politics in Florence usually fell along family lines, all the family members are of the same party usually, he's also basically asking what side are you on? In the factional conflicts in Florence, are you on my side? Are you on somebody else's side? So, here, where we might expect something that would unite, all we get is division, division socially and division politically.

Herzman: It's kind of interesting, in fact, Farinata seems to make the assumption here that because Dante is on the wrong side of all of these things that somehow that's better because it gives him the opportunity to show off. Essentially what he is doing is saying, "Ha, ha, all right, I'm better than you, my ancestors are better than you, and my party is better than you." All right? He says, just to prove it, "I had to scatter them, not once but twice." Well, this takes us back to that Guelf/Ghibelline struggle that we talked about in our introductory lectures.

Cook: It turns out Farinata is a Ghibelline in a city that was normally dominated by Guelfs, but twice in 1248 and in 1260, in fact, the Ghibellines did, as we know from our earlier lecture, temporarily kick out the Florentines, and it was during one of those periods when the Guelfs were kicked out when Dante, in fact, was born. So, he is correct in saying my party kicked out your party twice, going back to the good old days of 1248 and 1260.

Herzman: Now, it's interesting to see how Dante responds to this. The problem, again as we saw in the earlier lectures, if you happen to be somebody like Farinata who was a Ghibelline, is that that victory, or those victories, didn't last very long, and the Guelfs came back, and as subsequent history would have it, they came back permanently. Now, Dante knows this, and it's apparent that Farinata doesn't. So, here we have this "My old man can beat up your old man" kind of conversation going down in the middle of these tombs in the middle of this barren part of hell, and the thing that is very interesting is not simply that Farinata is baiting Dante, but that Dante is rising to the bait. So, Farinata is sort of there chalking up the victory points and Dante answers, Yes,

> 'They were expelled, but only to return
> from everywhere,' I said, 'not once but twice—
> an art your men, however, never mastered!'

So, from Dante's point of view, the pilgrim, it's kind of as though he's given a knockout punch to Farinata and Farinata's position. Your ancestors might be all these noble folks and all of that, but guess what? They're out of here, and they've not learned the art of coming back—ha, ha, ha.

Cook: Because, in fact, in 1300, when the poem is set, the Guelfs are in firm control, the Ghibellines have been not in power in Florence for more than 30 years, so Dante can trump the history card with the present card, if you will. It's also interesting to note that he refers to coming back from exile as an art. Isn't that an odd word to use to describe this kind of political maneuver? Really, we might think about the art of politics, and that's an appropriate term, but that's not the way that Farinata is using it. This art here is simply the muscle to kick out the fellow citizens of yours that for the minute you think of as the "bad guys."

Herzman: Now, at this point, there's kind of a suspension of the action here, and before we pick it up, just to sort of suggest that here what this tells us is as much about Dante as it does about Farinata in the sense that by 1300, or at 1300, when the poem is set, Dante, recently emerged from a dark wood of error, seems to be so caught up in partisan politics that he can't help but argue on Farinata's own level. That he's sort of doing exactly what Farinata is doing, but, of course, think about where it has gotten Farinata, and so, here you have Dante ready to go toe-to-toe with him, and drops him with a good right hand, but then another character appears who complicates issues by talking to Dante about something else.

Cook: What we find here is that another fellow occupant of the same tomb appears, not nearly as majestically as Farinata, but just sort of putting his chin over the edge of the tomb. It's an interesting contrast of these two souls who are going to be living eternally in this tomb, and he has a question for Dante, too.

Herzman: Tombmates from hell.

Cook:

> 'If it be great genius
>   that carries you along through this blind jail,
>   where is my son? Why is he not with you?'

Now there are a lot of ways in which this is an interesting question. First of all, does he have the right premise? Is Dante in hell because of Dante's great genius? Well, we know differently, of course, because we know that in some ways Dante's here because he's so messed up that without this journey he's going to be unable to be oriented toward God and away from self and sin, so we know that the premise has to be disputed, but given the premise, if you're here because it's some sort of reward for genius, where's my kid?

Herzman: It turns out that Dante, from this and from recognizing the guy as well, figures out that his kid turns out to be an old friend of Dante's, a fellow poet, obviously a fellow Florentine, and so Dante answers and says to him,

> 'that one waiting over there (that is, of course, to
> say, Virgil) guides me through here,
> the one, perhaps, your Guido held in scorn.'

Dante, in other words, is accepting the premise of this as of now unidentified speaker, and says, "Yeah, he doesn't like Virgil as much as I do, and that's why I'm here." So, Dante's kind of accepting the notion that he's there as a kind of reward rather than as sort of, as we've said, a shock, a sort of shock treatment for the soul.

Cook: Dante knows who this is. He tells us that he recognizes this soul from his positioning and from his question, so that's why he can answer specifically with the name of this man's son. But it's interesting to notice that Dante simply says this in the past tense as part of the conversation. Maybe your son's not along because he held Virgil in scorn, a very common way of speaking, but look at the way that this guy, whom we know is named Cavalcante, responds.

> Instantly he sprang to his full height and cried,
> 'What did you say? He *held*? Is he not living?
> The day's sweet light no longer strikes his eyes?'

When Dante pauses briefly before answering, because it turns out Guido is still alive, he falls back down into the tomb and we never see him again.

Herzman: So, here you have this person who essentially talks from the tomb in order to make mischief with Dante, misinterprets what Dante says, and goes back into the tomb before there's any response, and while Dante is sort of puzzling about this, a little slow on the uptake, and wasn't able to say, "No, no, no, your son is still living," we go back to the first conversation. It is this remarkable comedy of errors really that is being orchestrated down here. Farinata and Dante are talking, Cavalcante talks with Dante, Cavalcante disappears back into the tomb, Farinata picks up where he left off, and he picks up exactly where he left off. In other words, he picks up as if, not even as if, he picks up not recognizing the existence of the other person, and not recognizing any break in the conversation. He goes right back to what Dante had last said to him, namely the art of coming back after being kicked out of Florence, and says to Dante,

> he merely picked up where we left off:
>> 'If that art they did not master,' he went on,
>> 'that gives me greater pain than does this bed.
>
> But the face of the queen who reigns down here will glow
>> not more than fifty times before you learn
>> how hard it is to master such an art;'

Well, goodness gracious, what is going on there?

Cook: Remember, we've played the history card. That is to say, Farinata said, "My party beat up your party and kicked them out twice." Dante has played the present card, "Right now it is the Guelfs who are in power and not the Ghibellines. We're in and you guys are out." What is it, then, what's left? What card can Farinata play?

Herzman: It turns out he has a very nice trump card here; he has the future card, and what you have here is a very strong—perhaps the strongest in the Inferno—prediction of Dante's coming exile. The face of the queen who reigns down here in the darkness of hell, one never mentions the sun, so time is reckoned by the moon, and that "queen who reigns down here will glow / not more than fifty times," meaning fifty months will pass, before you learn how hard it is to master such an art, the art, remember, is the art of coming back after you've been kicked out. So, here we have in a very interesting, though very indirect way, a prediction of precisely what is going to happen to Dante down the road.

Cook: It's important to say, of course, that Dante is going to hear over and over again various hints about his exile, which takes place the year after the poem is set, but he won't have it sort of laid out flat, clear and unequivocally, until he gets all the way to heaven, another reminder that we simply can't take Inferno and go home and say we understand what Dante's about and how the *Commedia* works.

Herzman: Notice also this is a nifty way of showing by example how it is important that we keep in mind all the time the difference between the poem when it was written and the poem as it's set as a journey. Dante, the poet, is constructing this in exile, all right? The pilgrim, at the height of his own political power, hears essentially a prediction of that exile. From the point of view of the poet it's history, from the point of view of the pilgrim it's prophecy. So, one of the advantages of setting the poem in 1300 then becomes all the ways in which Dante is able to use the history between 1300 and the time he writes the poem as a kind of prediction of the future.

Cook: After this past-present-future argument takes place, Farinata has some questions, still more questions, in fact, to ask Dante. "Why is it that your party, the Guelfs, are so tough on my family?" Because, what we know is that in 1280 the Ghibellines were allowed to come back to Florence from exile. They weren't given power, but they were literally allowed to move back into the city. The one exception was the family of Farinata. Farinata was, by that time, dead. "Why are you guys so tough on my family? Why don't you let them back in, too?" It's an interesting question, and Dante answers this way.

> …'The massacre and butchery
> that stained the waters of the Arbia red
> now cause such laws to issue from our councils.'

Herzman: Well, "the massacre and the butchery / that stained the waters of the Arbia red," once again, goes back to that year 1260 that we've already seen in this canto. That was one of the times that his ancestors scattered Dante's ancestors because that was to folks then—and, if you're Siennese, even now—the Battle of Montaperti, the famous Battle of Montaperti, in which a combination of Siennese forces and Ghibelline traitors in Florence allied to defeat the main army of Florence. Farinata was chief among the traitors, and it took place at a place called Montaperti, where a little tiny stream called the Arbia was died red with the blood of those who died fighting there. So, by this time, it's not like the memory has been forgotten. I even own a T-shirt that says "Remember Montaperti" on it, so you can imagine that if that's true in 2001, what it would have been like in 1300, and so Dante is saying, "Look, the reason that we don't like you so much is because you betrayed your city, and betrayal is not just some sort of abstract thing that happens, betrayal is lots of us being killed."

Cook: Let's talk about how this betrayal happened. Remember Farinata has already told us what he values: me, my family, and my party. Well, those are parts of reality, but, of course, Farinata also has some things in common with Dante: fellow Florentine, fellow Italian, fellow Christian, fellow human. Farinata doesn't list any of those things; he only listed the things that divide, and what's interesting here is that Farinata and his family and his party were in the minority; they were not in power in Florence, okay? So, what does he do? He goes to Siena which was a Ghibelline city at the time, makes an alliance with Siena, the neighbor and enemy to the south of Florence, saying bring all the Ghibellines of Florence to fight alongside you guys when we take on my fellow Florentines who are not Ghibellines. So, think about this, why is your city so harsh toward my family? Because you are a traitor. Because you sold out Florence because party, Ghibelline, meant more than city, or nation we would say today, Florence. How's that for a pretty good reason for the Florentines being sort of harsh on the family of Farinata?

Herzman: Of course, like everybody else in hell, Farinata doesn't want to take blame, he can't; finds a very interesting way of shifting responsibility here. He sighed. He's got all of the political gestures down.

> He sighed, shaking his head. 'It was not I
> > alone took part,' (I did not do it all by myself) nor certainly
> would I have joined the rest without good cause.'

Well, one wonders exactly what the good cause is, and I think that, in fact, Farinata kind of explains it in the immediate next tercet.

> 'But I alone stood up when all of them
> > were ready to have Florence razed. It was I
> who openly stood up in her defense.'

What he's doing, of course, is saying that he was maybe not patriotic according to most Guelf standards, but here you go, they wanted to tear down the city stone by stone. "The Siennese realized full well that they weren't going to have this opportunity all that often, and they said, 'We've got them now, so let's just do them in,' and I wouldn't let them do that. I stood up as the lone voice of truth and justice and the Florentine way, and spoke for Florence's defense." Again, a great patriot? Well, maybe not.

Cook: Perhaps simply self-serving. After all, this is a guy who wanted to rule. This is a guy who betrayed his country in order to try to rule it, and now his allies are saying, "Why don't we tear the place down?" So, although here he's saying what a patriot I was, what a savior of Florence I was, I think we can also hear him saying, "I want to rule this place, it's all about me. It's about me, my family, and my party. You take Florence out and you tear down my house.

You get rid of my family. You don't give me the fruits of victory, which is power. Not the power to do justice, not the power to care for Florence and its citizens, simply power for power's sake," and we need to hear that even though we don't literally hear the words as Farinata is telling this story.

By the way, it's important to say that Farinata was sort of the co-victor in this battle along with the head of the Siennese Ghibellines, whose name is Provenzan Salvani. You might expect, after all, since Dante is a Guelf, and Provenzan Salvani and Farinata are Ghibellines, that probably Dante's got a pretty good place for this Siennese enemy down in hell, too. Well, we're going to meet Provenzan Salvani. We're going to meet him on the road to heaven. We're going to meet him in purgatory. He's among the saved. This is not about Guelfs and Ghibellines, per se. This is about something much more fundamental. It's about what you value and the way you divide, rather than unite.

Herzman: Well, one of the things that sort of continues is this notion of division. Dante asks a question of Farinata, "How come you could tell about the future? That seems odd." Farinata's answer is, "We have a kind of faulty vision down here. We can't see what's present; we can't see what's in front of us; we can only see what's at a distance." Now, that's a really neat trick to have, but notice it's not a trick that they're going to be able to keep up for very long because once time comes to a halt, in other words, once the Last Judgment is there, there won't be that future at all, they'll only be able to see the present, and what they'll be able to see is exactly and precisely nothing. So, in a way, it's something that is both a poetic device for the pilgrim to get info, but also it says something about the nature of the punishment itself. Now, notice that Dante sort of continues with all of this. He says,

> 'Thus, you can understand (Farinata speaking) how all of our knowledge
> will be completely dead at the time when
> the door to the future things is closed forever.'

Dante comes back and he says,

> Then, I, moved by regret for what I had done,
> said, 'Now will you please tell the fallen one
> his son is still on earth among the living?'

Remember that intermediate speaker, that Cavalcante guy, said, "My son, how come he is not here?" assumes that Dante is saying that he is dead, simply a bad mistake in grammar. Dante wants Farinata to fix it for him, but what we've seen in the dramatic interchange between the two of them here, is that Farinata and Cavalcante don't so much as recognize each other's existence. They're stuck in the same tomb for all eternity, and they simply refuse to recognize that the other one exists. So, what Dante is asking is never going to happen, but notice also this is a nifty way for the poet to talk about what happens when you take this idea of partisan politics and push it as far as it will go.

Cook: That brings us back to the question that we raised at the beginning: "Why, in the circle of the heretics, do we talk about politics and poetry at all? Why is that the appropriate topic?" Well, if we think about it, first of all, there is a lot of pride and a lot of factionalism, if you will, in politics and poetry. Why is Farinata so intense about his family? Is it because of justice? Is it because it is his family? Is Cavalcante really a careful reader of poetry and therefore knows that his son is as good a poet as Dante? Or is it just the fact that "it's my son"? We have these divisions in both of these characters in the realm of the arts, we might say more generally, and in the art of politics, and isn't that what heresy really is? In many ways, a good theological definition of heresy would be taking a part of the truth and assuming it's the whole truth, and not letting anything else affect that, and if that becomes a pretty good definition—not quite a textbook definition—of heresy, isn't that exactly what we're seeing here in Farinata, in Cavalcante, and in Dante the pilgrim?

Herzman: So, here you have this wonderful canto in which, unlike, let's say, Francesca, where the subject among the lustful is lust, the subject is politics and poetry, but in fact, everything they say embodies the nature of heresy, and gives us a kind of interesting commentary on it, as well as to suggest to us that whether or not Dante the pilgrim ever had a problem with formal heresy in any theological sense, this notion of partisanship was something that affected him very strongly, and that he needs very, very greatly to overcome.

Cook: So, now, we head down a little but further, into the area of the sins of violence.

Lecture Eight
The Seventh Circle—The Violent

Scope:

In this lecture, we will examine two different examples of violence: suicide and sodomy. According to Dante's classifications, violence, the seventh circle of hell, is subdivided according to its object. Violence can be directed to others, to self, or to God. According to Dante's scheme, sodomy belongs with violence against God, because it is a sin against nature, the "offspring" of God. In the wood of the suicides, in Canto 13, we encounter Pier delle Vigne, who was "chief of staff" to the Emperor Frederick II and killed himself when he fell from favor. Dante must learn from Pier, because in his exile he will experience a similar fall from favor. In Inferno 15, Dante meets his old teacher, Brunetto Latini, who praises Dante as his star pupil. Brunetto encourages Dante to seek earthly fame, and in that advice one sees by analogy the nature of sodomy—making something barren that ought to be fruitful.

Outline

I. Dante's classification of sins of violence, the seventh circle, is complex and, because it is different from modern notions, instructive.

    A. He explains this classification in Canto 11.

    B. Violence is classified according to its object.

        1. Violence can be directed against others, self, and God.

        2. Violence against God includes blasphemy.

        3. It also includes the sins of sodomy and usury.

        4. These are directed against God's "child," nature, and God's "grandchild," art.

II. The wood of the suicides, Canto 13, is another good place to observe Dante's "spiritual geography."

    A. It is defined by images of negation and by harsh and barren shrubbery.

    B. The souls themselves have been turned into shrubs, who can only talk by having one of their branches broken.

C. They have lost self-determination in hell, just as they have given up self-determination with their sin.

III. Dante listens to the spurting branch of Pier delle Vigne, "chief of staff" to the Emperor Frederick II, who "writes" what is in effect a posthumous suicide note.

    A. Pier talks about his loyalty and fidelity to Frederick.

    B. He blames his fall, and his suicide, on the envy of the court.

    C. His description is especially self-serving.

    D. He uses highly charged religious language to describe the relationship between himself and Frederick, a heretic who is himself in the Inferno (cf. Canto 10).

    E. Suicide becomes at once a self-justification and a way of getting even with his enemies.

IV. Because of Dante's own "future" fall from political power, this is a particularly powerful "ghost of Christmas future" for Dante.

    A. It is not an accident that this canto also takes place in a "dark wood."

    B. Dante, too, will have to deal with the powerlessness of exile, separated from the "body politic" of his native Florence.

    C. Pier's behavior is an especially strong example of how not to act in exile and, thus, an especially strong warning to Dante. Whether or not Dante himself was literally tempted by suicide, he was certainly tempted by the selfish, despairing attitude that Pier represents.

V. In Canto 15, we encounter violence against God in the form of sodomy.

    A. As in the discussion of heresy, the literal sin is not discussed directly.

    B. But the geography at the beginning of the canto, much of it drawn from the opening of Genesis, directs our attention to the biblical concept of being fruitful and multiplying.

VI. Dante has a conversation with his old teacher, the poet, rhetorician, and Guelf leader Brunetto Latini.

    A. Brunetto recognizes Dante as his star pupil and encourages him to "follow his star." Brunetto is really thinking of his own fame.

B. Brunetto's seductive argument on the nature of fame helps to suggest the nature of sodomy by analogy: Brunetto is suggesting that fame is a kind of idol, a false form of eternal life.

C. A barren earthly fame becomes an analogous way of talking about sodomy.

D. Just as in his talk with Francesca da Rimini Dante learned that there are false and dangerous types of reading, so in his colloquy with Brunetto he learns that there are dangerous ways of writing.

E. Brunetto's discourse is also connected to important ideas of free will and determinism.

Readings:

Dante, *Inferno*, Cantos 11–15.

Robert Hollander, *Allegory in Dante's Commedia*, Chapter 1.

Questions to Consider:

1. Why is Pier's sin so important for Dante to learn about, given the prophecies that have already been made of his exile from Florence?

2. Pier claims that he has been faithful to his lord. Does he have the "right" lord in mind?

3. Why is the fifteenth canto, where sodomites are punished, a place where Dante talks about the misuse of the gift of language?

Lecture Eight—Transcript
The Seventh Circle—The Violent

Cook: We visited Francesca in the area of incontinence, and then we met Farinata and Cavalcante in what Ron described as a kind of transition, that heresy doesn't fit neatly in the basic categories of sin, but once we leave them we move into the area of violence, the second of the three major categories of sin. Dante does something a little bit different here because while for each of the kinds of incontinence there is a separate circle—circles two, three, four, and five—when we get to the violent, all the different kinds of violence are in one circle and the circle itself is subdivided. Basically, the subdivisions work this way: There are three different objects, if you will, of violence. You can be violent against neighbors. So, you can be a murderer, for example, or you can plunder somebody's property. You can be violent against self. That would include the suicides. Or, you can be violent against God, and that would include blasphemers and others. So there are these three sort of sub-categories. It's actually even a little more complicated than that, but that's the way we'll get started. So, what we're going to do is look at two different interludes, two different events, in two of these three subdivisions of the circle of violence. We're going to first go to the suicides—which is Inferno 13—and then we're going to go to the part of circle seven that deals with the sodomites, Canto 15.

Herzman: Now, the whole notion of suicide is a very tricky one, both I think from a modern and a medieval perspective, but it's interesting to see this is another one of those places where hints about the nature of the sin can be picked up by taking a look at the geography that's created at the beginning of the cantos. In other words, this is another one of those places as it was with Francesca and the lustful where there is a very telling "spiritual geography" that is presented for us. What we find is that there is this sort of barren, I'm going to make a bad pun, shrub-section. It's a subsection of the circle of violence with a lot of grubby shrubs there, and the way in which these shrubs are described is quite interesting. The beginning of the canto goes this way:

> Not yet had Nessus reached the other side
> when we were on our way into a forest
> that was not marked by any path at all.

No green leaves, but rather black in color,
　　no smooth branches, but twisted and entangled,
　　no fruit, but thorns of poison bloomed instead.

No thick, rough, scrubby home like this exists—
　　not even between Cecina and Corneto—
　　for those wild beasts that hate the run of farmland.

Well, even the mildly perceptive listener could figure out there were a lot of no's there, a lot of not's, a lot of—as we would say nowadays—a lot of negativity coming through. So that in a way it's described and defined by what's not there, by a kind of negation, and that becomes clue number one, and a very important clue, to what we're dealing with in the wood of the suicides.

Cook: We need to think about this negativity, as Ron so well described it, because if we ask ourselves how Dante viewed human life, one clear way, drawing in the Judeo-Christian tradition, is that it's a gift from God. It is something that God gives to us. Suicide is saying no thanks. Suicide is giving back, turning down, rejecting the gift, and therefore this bombardment with those no words—each of the first three tercets begins with one of those no words—is a way of saying something about the essence of suicide.

Herzman: It turns out that these grubby shrubs are themselves the suicides. That's what they've been transformed into. Begin thinking about what the appropriateness of that is, the sense that Dante has that there's a correspondence between sin and punishment. It involves the kind of negativity that we just talked about, but it also involves a sense that in suicide what you do is you sort of give up your fight to self-determination, and so by becoming these shrubs in this sort of grubby part of hell, what happens is that they are no longer capable of any kind of self-determination, and that even includes the fact that they have to wait until somebody comes along and tears off a branch to provide an opening through which they can speak. So, even their ability to communicate has been—in a way—taken away from them, and, of course, it has been taken away from them by their own actions. Anyhow, Dante and Virgil come along, snap off a twig, and begin to have one of the most interesting conversations in hell.

Cook: This shrub starts speaking, as Ron suggested, because Dante breaks off this branch, by the way, quite offended that somebody broke off one of his branches. "Why are you doing that to me?" The obvious answer being, I suppose, you are a shrub. But, at any rate, this is what he says as he identifies himself,

> 'I am the one who held both of the keys
>   that fitted Frederick's heart; I turned them both,
>   locking and unlocking, with such finesse
>
> that I let few into his confidence.'

By those words he identifies himself. He's a fellow named Pier delle Vigne, which literally means "Peter of the vines," and he was—we would perhaps today say—the "chief of staff" to the Holy Roman Emperor Frederick II, who died in 1250. He was the guy who controlled who got two minutes, who got five minutes, and who got no minutes with the Emperor Frederick II. You may recall from some of our political background that Frederick II was that great fighter against the papacy for control of Italy. He died in 1250, and it's important to say that he's already been mentioned as a character in hell at the end of Canto 10 where we met Farinata and Cavalcante, when we have that sort of introduction around (who else is here) we're told that Frederick II is there. So, whatever he says about his boss, keep in mind, we know where his boss is.

Herzman: Yes, so he was boss to a heretic, and his job, as Bill said, is access "chief of staff." He was also, again to use the modern parlance, a bit of a spin-doctor for Frederick. That is to say one of the things, and this may certainly have influenced Dante's placement of Frederick with the heretics, one of the things that Frederick did was to promulgate the idea that as kind of a successor to the Roman Emperors it would be a really nifty thing if they reinstituted the idea of Emperor worship, and the person that was sort of responsible for the cult of Frederick, that is to say, the person who was the propaganda man for that cult, was none other than Pier delle Vigne. So, his own writings would talk about Frederick in terms that were sort of using language of Roman courts, but also using language kind of taken from Christianity but devoid of their Christian content and made to apply to Frederick himself. So, that's the job he had, and a very fine job it was up to a point because the short version of the story is that he was sort of hounded from office by people who were envious of him, and then when he was removed from office, he thought that the only way to deal with that was, well, by killing himself. That's the story that he tells us. Again, like the other souls in hell, in a very self-serving way, in a way that puts the blame on somebody else, in a way that needs to be followed very carefully to see where things are there that they don't really realize they're saying to us.

Cook: He's also very interesting to us because he said, "No matter what the accusations were at court, I never broke faith with my lord." Of course, the lord he had in mind was Frederick II. He forgets the bigger picture. He did break faith with his Lord; we would say with a capital L, Lord, the Lord God, his creator. So, he has a very limited view of things, and for him if it was not part of this political scheme, this political power, it simply doesn't exist. There is no higher authority than Frederick II, whom, again, we know is a heretic who is in a flaming tomb in hell.

Herzman: Let's listen to his language for a minute.

> …'So appealing are your lovely words, (he says to Dante)
> I must reply. Be not displeased if I
> am lured into a little conversation.'

Funny language for a shrub, by the way, which is to say he's speaking with all of the elegance and all of the kind of strutting that he had when he still had that position, even though even access to speech itself is denied him unless somebody breaks off a branch.

> 'I am the one who held both of the keys
> that fitted into Frederick's heart; I turned them both,
> locking and unlocking, with such finesse
>
> that I let few into his confidence.
> I was so faithful to my glorious office,
> I lost not only sleep but life itself.'

In other words, he's suggesting that you didn't have to live in the 21st century to be a workaholic, that he lost not only sleep, but life itself because he never wavered in his faithfulness to his boss, and then he says,

> 'That courtesan (at court that's what they're called, anyhow)
> who constantly surveyed
> Caesar's household with her adulterous eyes,
> mankind's undoing, the special vice of the courts,
>
> Inflamed the hearts of everyone against me,
> and these inflamed, inflamed in turn Augustus,

Notice that he is calling his Emperor Frederick Caesar, he's calling him Augustus.

> and my happy honors turned to sad laments.

> My mind, moved by scornful satisfaction,
>> believing that death would free me from all scorn,
>> made me unjust to me, who was all just.

I did my job, did it right, never wavered, so I killed myself.

> By the strange roots of my own tree I swear
>> to you that never once did I break faith
>> with my lord, who was so worthy of all honor.'

Again, our point is, as Bill pointed out, we ought to be a little bit skeptical.

> 'If one of you should go back to the world,
>> restore the memory of me, who here
>> remain cut down by the blow that Envy gave.'

So, at the end of this rhetorically florid little speech of his, we find out that that courtesan that he talks about at the beginning turns out to be envy. Once again, shift the blame on someone or somebody else. "Envy was the one who was responsible for my death." Notice, in effect, what Pier is saying about the nature of suicide. I don't mind playing the game when I'm winning; when I'm not winning, I'm not playing anymore. In other words, the sense that life is only to be lived on the terms that I establish. Once I don't have that position of power, I'll show them all, I'm just not going to play at all, and in that Dante the poet is getting to the essence of what suicide is all about.

Cook: This is so important because, let's remember, that although the poem is set in 1300, Dante has already heard the prediction that he's going to be kicked out of Florence That is to say, he is actually elected a prior about two months after this poem takes place, but he's going to be kicked out the next year. So, we can imagine Dante in the situation analogous to Pier's. I got to play for the first 35 years with life in my terms, now I'm out and I didn't get back. We know that because the prediction is he will not come back from exile. Farinata made that prediction. So, we can understand why this is a particularly important conversation for Dante the pilgrim, why he has a lot to learn here, why Dante the poet makes this such a dramatic and carefully crafted episode because this is one that really gets to the heart of something that Dante himself is going to have to face up to. Is life worth living when it isn't going well? Is life worth living when almost all the givens of that life have been pulled out from underneath me?

Herzman: We don't know, of course, whether suicide in any literal sense was a temptation to Dante after he was sent into exile, but certainly the attitude that leads to it most certainly was. The idea that I'm not playing at all if I can't play on my own terms, and given the fact that all of Pier's sort of lifetime accomplishments kind of add up to Dante's own, this civil servant who was also a defender of empire, let's not forget, as was Dante himself, unjustly condemned—or at least as Pier would think—by a government that he served. In seeing Pier, this is one of the best examples of Dante seeing a "ghost of Christmas future." It's really nifty to see the way in which once again Dante, sort of being sympathetic to Pier's plight, is really being sympathetic to something that is going to happen to him later on; if he takes Pier's route, he'll wind up exactly where Pier is now.

Cook: As we turn to the second place we're going to stop in the area of violence, on the surface it will not seem like it is nearly as relevant to the personal story of Dante the pilgrim as the place we've just been, because it is the canto where we meet the sodomites, who are violent against God, or more literally Dante says, violent against nature, which is the "child" of God. Since we know that Dante was, in fact, not a homosexual and not tempted into homosexual relationships, it seems that this would be a canto that would largely just sort of be a place where he's spending a little time, learning a little detached information, and then moving on to something else that is perhaps more relevant to him. But, in fact, Dante crafts this canto with such care that like in Canto 10, the discussion is not about the most literal definition of the sin, but it's broader so that Dante the pilgrim has to learn (and a lot to learn) from the sinner he encounters, his old mentor we would say, Brunetto Latini.

Herzman: In setting this up, let's remind ourselves of what we are dealing with here. This is violence against God, what does that mean? One of the problems is that it's easy to just sort of simply literally think about what it means to be violent against neighbor, bang—you're dead, violence against self—suicide, but God is a different take, a different read, because you can't be violent against God in that same physical way. God doesn't have that kind of existence. So, it's pretty clear that the first category, the previous canto, blasphemy, is the way you do it directly. What you see in the canto of the blasphemers, quite literally, is a sinner giving God the finger. So, you have blasphemy as violence against God in that sense. But here, sodomy, violence against God, it's harder to figure out, and the clue is that you have to look at God not only in himself, but in terms of what God has left for us—his own creation. So, in a sense, by being violent against God's creation, you're being violent against God even though it's not a direct kick to God in the slacks, or sticking him in the bellybutton with a knife. Dante, I think, would expect that his audience would see this from a very important passage at the beginning of the Book of Genesis. We're told that we're in the image and likeness of God, and we're told that God tells us to be fruitful and multiply, and we're meant to put those two ideas together.

Cook: After all, if you think about how we imitate God, what are the things we know from Genesis? One is that God brings order out of chaos, and in the medieval understanding of Genesis I it means that humans are to go ahead and carry forth that call, that act, in imitation of God. So, for example, we might clear stones and plow a field so that that field produces food. That would be continuing the process of ordering. Now, as it turns out, that is a very useful notion because I want you to listen to the way Dante describes the place where the sodomites are punished.

> As the Flemings, living with their constant threat
> of flood, takes tides rushing in between Wissant
> and Bruges, build their dikes to force the sea back;
>
> as the Paduans build theirs on the shore of Brenta
> to protect their town and homes before warm
> weather
> turns Chiarentana's snow into rushing water—
>
> so were these walls we walked upon constructed,

In other words, as Dante often does, he says, "Let me tell you what I saw down in hell by linking it to something on earth." What he links it to are images of art, of art in the medieval sense, of continuing the process of ordering. These are both examples of people who have water that is destructive, whether it's the sea in the first example or a river in the second, and so humans build dikes and levies to hold the water back so that the crops aren't flooded and so that the land produces. So, in other words, God has given humans the power of continuing the process of ordering, and they order so that creation bears fruit and provides sustenance for human beings.

Herzman: So, what we're going to start to think about is various ways in which the idea, the concept of being fruitful and multiplying—or of ordering—turns out to be the subject of this canto, even though on the surface we seem to be talking about something different once again. The idea of sodomy itself, for example, is not brought up directly in the cantos. There are a couple of indirect suggestions that that is what is going on here, but here you have Dante meeting an old teacher of his, and mostly what they talk about is the potential in Dante's career to really be kind of the star pupil of all time, of this person who is identified as Brunetto Latini, in fact, a famous rhetorician and teacher of the previous generation.

Cook: So, we're down here in something that sort of reminds Dante of this beautiful—keeping the water out so that the crops will grow, except where the sodomites are is a burning desert with fire coming down. In other words, what Dante has done is taken an image on earth that is fruitful and turned it into an image of barrenness. It's the barrenness of the geography contrasting with his earthly analogs that so strikes us, and begins to give us a handle on dealing with how to understand the conversation between Dante and Brunetto Latini. Think about this phrase: taking something that's meant to be fruitful and using it in a way that's barren. That may be literally true about sexual reproduction. It is true about our work as artists on earth, again clearing a field or whatever. Down here the opposite must have been what Brunetto did, because his punishment is to live in a barren parody of that on earth.

Herzman: The introduction, that is to say, the meeting of the two, is sort of interesting in terms of the recognition. Dante sees these folks walking by; they are being pelted with burning flames as they walk around this sort of sandy desert, very barren thing here. Again, there's a sense in which all of the sub-circles of the violence have a kind of barren geography to them. He sees this, and he recognizes,

> Eyed in such a way by this strange crew,
>   I was recognized by one of them, who grabbed
>   my garment's hem and shouted, 'How marvelous!'

And I, when he reached out his arm toward me,
    straining my eyes, saw through his face's crust,
    through his burned features that could not prevent

my memory from bringing back his name;
    and bending my face down to meet with his,
    I said: 'Is this really you, here, Ser Brunetto?'

Cook: That would be Brunetto Latini who had just died six years before the poem is set. Brunetto Latini was a rhetorician, as Ron said, a poet, and also a very important political figure, a Guelf as it turns out who was exiled in 1260 after the Battle of Montaperti. When Dante refers to him as his teacher, we think historically not so much that Dante sort of formally studied under him, but rather he was sort of a role model for Dante, the successful politician, the successful poet, the great user of language in both of those vocations where precise and careful use of language is so important.

Herzman: Again, this seems to be this sort of reciprocal arrangement where both are recognizing the debt that they have to the other. Brunetto's language, "'Oh my son, may it not displease you… My son,'" he said, "'…I shall follow at your hem / and then rejoin my family.'" All the language that he is using to talk to Dante is rather ironic because he's here for a sin that doesn't really allow for his having literal sons, but it also points to the fact that what he's seeing in Dante, many teachers see this in their students, you're my student and you're my metaphorical child. My students are my metaphorical children. So he's talking about and to Dante in that way, but it's sort of clear that he sees in Dante something very special as well in Dante's talent and in Dante's abilities. So, what he does is he sort of says, "How come you're here?" What he says is very interesting. "…'What fortune or what destiny / leads you down here before your final hour?'" A question that a lot of people are asking—indirectly at any rate—What are you doing here, you're not dead? The rest of us are dead. Again, Dante says, this is the first time that he gets it even partially right, he's here now because he's gone astray in the previous life, that is to say gone astray up there. Brunetto takes this as a very interesting sign that Dante is meant to make it to the top, as though this were somehow an episode in that old, it's not exactly a sitcom, the TV show *Fame*, and we're going to see the most famous of all. I'm going to make it to the top, yes sir, Dante Alighieri. Take a look at what he says to him, "He said to me:

'Follow your constellation / and you cannot fail to reach your port of glory.'" Kid, your name is gonna be in lights.

Cook: In fact, the next line is also interesting, "'not if I saw clearly in the happy life;'" meaning when I was alive back on earth. Well, this is a guy down in hell with flames falling on him in a barren desert, saying, "If I saw things really right back in the world, you've got it made. I saw your talents, I saw your brilliance, and I really would have done everything to push you forward had I still been alive." Now, on the one hand that can sound like a good thing for a mentor to say, "I really thought you had it. I want you to get ahead." All of that has been said many times by us to our students, but there's another side to this. We also both know the danger of saying, "Boy, I have this student who graduated who is now a (fill in the blank), and if this person becomes famous enough, you know, Oprah's going to call me up and say do you want to be on this show and talk about what it was like to be the college professor of so and so?" That it's very easy to slip from I'm doing it for them to I'm doing it for me, and I think there's reason that Brunetto has made that move, and Brunetto is really talking about Dante's fame in light of the fact that it will enhance his own fame.

Herzman: Notice, of course, what is implicated there is that what he is saying to Dante is, if you "follow your constellation / you cannot fail to reach your port of glory." Well, that means from Brunetto's point of view, that your name is going to be in lights. Dante's not taking this journey so that his name will be in lights. He's taking this journey to get out of this moral swamp that he's in, and in the process, he's going to take this journey that's going to lead him to see God, to the vision of God face to face, but he's doing that so that he can actually go back and take that journey again when he dies. In other words, the answer to life is not fame down here on earth. That if you look for that to the exclusion of other more important things, what you're doing is—in a very real way—failing to be fruitful and multiply. What you're doing in a very real way is sort of cutting yourself off from the larger reality of fruitfulness that is the goal of all humans, but that Dante has to relearn himself. To put it another way, of course, if Dante were to follow Brunetto's advice, then it's highly likely that Dante would wind up here with Brunetto, and it seems to me that this is the way in which Brunetto is sort of revealing himself far greater than he realizes.

Cook: Dante the pilgrim—at least seeing him before—sort of falls into this trap. After all, this is a very attractive thing to hear from a senior to you, a mentor, a famous person. In fact, Dante says, "Gosh, Brunetto, I wish you weren't dead yet because you were the one who was teaching me how to make myself eternal. You were my mentor, my guide, on making myself eternal." Well, what a funny thing to say to a guy who is down here with fire dripping down on him for all of eternity. Dante doesn't quite get it. Again, on the surface we might say, "Gee, making yourself eternal sounds like a pretty good thing to learn," but what does Brunetto teach him about how to make himself eternal? Brunetto himself gives us a clue because at the end when this conversation sort of terminates, and they wave goodbye to one another, Brunetto says, "'Remember my *Trésor*,' (a book he wrote) 'where I live on.'" Making yourself eternal is all about getting yourself famous. My eternal life comes from the fact I wrote this famous thing, and this is a great danger to a genius like Dante.

Herzman: It's also interesting, I suppose that a case could be made that maybe one of these days Brunetto Latini's studies are going to come back and a lot of people are going to want to study his works for his own sake, but by and large when people read works like Brunetto's *Trésor* nowadays, they read them so they can find out some more about Dante, and it's sort of interesting if you think about it from that perspective. Dante is the one who gets the fame, but paradoxically he gets it because he has to learn how to write for different reasons and different purposes. If you're looking for the fame, then you become a footnote to somebody else. It's also interesting if you think about this, if you go back to Francesca, with Francesca Dante had to learn that there were wrong ways to read, per diletto. Now what he's learning is that there are wrong reasons for writing, and in a sense, in his embodiment of them, as somebody down there in hell, Brunetto presents a lesson in wrong reasons for writing.

Cook: Now what we're going to do is leave the circle of the violent and enter into the very deepest part of hell, the third major subdivision. Beginning with the next lecture, we're going to take a look at sinners who are guilty of a category of sin we call fraud.

Lecture Nine
The Sin of Simony

Scope:

The third major category of sin in Dante's Inferno is fraud. In this lecture, we examine one of the most interesting and illustrative examples of fraud: the buying and selling of church offices, known as simony. Dante the writer has the audacity to use as examples of this sin the popes of his own time, whom he did not hesitate to condemn because of their simoniac practices. In addition to Nicholas III, who is the pope that the pilgrim encounters buried upside down in the rock at the bottom of the ditch, the poet condemns Boniface VIII—the pope responsible for Dante's exile from Florence—for this sin through an imaginative prediction of his fate in the afterlife. In this canto, Dante is concerned with all the ways in which spiritual ideals are inverted by those who use spiritual office for material gain. This canto is especially important in the structure of the Inferno, because we can see Dante the pilgrim's growth in knowledge as he responds with prophetic anger to the sin, denouncing it in a stirring harangue at the end of the canto.

Outline

I. The eighth circle of the Inferno deals with fraud, a general name for all the sins of the (misguided) intellect.

   A. This circle is divided into ten ditches, called *bolgias* by Dante.

   B. Each of these ten ditches contains a different kind of fraud.

   C. Fraud seems especially concerned with the destruction of possibilities for community. Dante is telling us not only about a personal vice but about a threat to all human society.

   D. Fraud is also concerned with perversions of language and speech.

   E. For example, we see flatterers in the second *bolgia*.

II. In the third *bolgia* are found the simoniacs, those guilty of perverting their spiritual office by buying and selling church offices.

    A. Dante seems to signal that simony is an especially reprehensible sin by the poet's stirring invocation at the beginning.

    B. He addresses the followers of Simon Magus, or Simon the Magician, who tried to buy the gifts of the spirit in Acts of the Apostles 8.

    C. The followers of Simon Magus are buried upside down in rock in hell, imitating the fall of Simon Magus as depicted in medieval art. Flames burn their upended feet in an inversion of the flame of the Holy Spirit that descended on the heads of Christ's apostles at Pentecost.

    D. Simon Magus is an inversion of the ideal presented by Simon Peter, the first pope.

    E. We see examples of inversion of the spiritual throughout the canto.

    F. Dante describes what he sees here by comparing it to the baptismal font at the baptistery of his native Florence.

        1. He describes an incident from his youth that took place at the baptismal font there, exonerating himself from an accusation of desecration of church property. Dante had apparently smashed a baptismal font to save someone from drowning in it.

        2. In the process, he gives us a clue to the nature of the sin and to his purpose in calling the church to account for its spiritual failures.

        3. He is "tearing down in order to build up," in the manner of a biblical prophet—poetically taking a hammer to abuses in the Church to remove threats to its life.

III. Dante has an extended encounter with a figure whose legs stick out of the rock, a colloquy in which the pilgrim, in effect, imitates a priest hearing the confession of a hired assassin—a type of criminal who, in Florence, was punished by being buried alive upside down.

A. At first, Dante is confused, because the figure misidentifies Dante, mistaking him for Pope Boniface VIII (r. 1294–1303), whose place in hell is thereby predicted.

    1. Boniface is alive in 1300, the fictional date of the journey.

    2. Boniface will be recalled by other figures in hell as well.

    3. Boniface is the person most responsible for the poet's own exile.

B. The figure identifies himself as Pope Nicholas III (r. 1277–1280), a Roman Orsini, or "son of the she-bear."

C. Nicholas presents Dante with his "confession" of nepotism and greed. He admits that, even after putting on "the great mantle" of the papacy, he cared more for his family's interests than the good of the whole Church.

D. He also predicts the fate of Clement V (d. 1314), thus presenting an infernal papal trinity, all of whom will wind up buried forever head-down in rock, in keeping with their sins.

E. The whole scene is a "Confession," with the pilgrim Dante as a priest and Nicholas as a false penitent who isn't really sorry for the wrong he has done.

IV. The pilgrim responds with a stinging harangue condemning the sin.

A. In this harangue, the pilgrim sounds like the poet does at the beginning of the canto—the pilgrim is beginning to see that hell is a place of justice.

B. Thus, we are able to see how much the pilgrim has learned, perhaps for the first time in the poem. He grasps the pervasive corruption wrought by simony.

C. The language of his condemnation is drawn in part from the Book of Revelation, relating the simony of the popes to the evils of the Last Days.

D. The canto also echoes passages from the Acts of the Apostles, showing the holy life and actions of Saint Peter as the ideal that these simoniac popes—Peter's successors—have perverted.

E. Dante ponders whether the Constantinian establishment of the Church was a wise move.

Readings:

Bible, Acts of the Apostles, Chapters 1–4, 8.

Dante, *Inferno*, Canto 16–19.

Questions to Consider:

1. How do we see the growth of Dante the pilgrim in his encounter with Nicholas III?

2. Why does Dante tell what appears to be the self-indulgent tale about smashing the baptismal font in Florence?

3. How does Dante the poet tell his readers to pay special attention to what he writes in this canto?

Lecture Nine—Transcript
The Sin of Simony

Herzman: You'll recall that the Inferno is divided into three major subdivisions—incontinence, violence, and fraud—and that we dealt with several examples of violence in previous lectures and said that they were all part of one circle, circle seven. Well, in the nine-circle structure of the Inferno then, we have two more to go, and both of those are concerned with the third major category, the sins connected with fraud. Remember that these are sins connected with misguided intellect. That, what Dante does here is deal with all of the ways in which our capacity for wisdom as human beings is perverted, turned upside down, ruined, and he's also particularly concerned with the large social implications of this kind of sin, the failure to achieve community, or the way these sins destroy community.

His way of setting this up for the eighth circle is to have a series of concentric ditches, called *bolgias* in Italian, and in each of these ten ditches, we have examples of the sin of fraud. Now, again, as was true with our discussion of incontinence and our discussion of violence, what we're going to do is look at representative examples and sort of suggest to you that what we say about them would be a really big help in reading the other *bolgias* on your own. We're going to start by talking about one of the most interesting and one of the most consequential of the sins of fraud, what was called in the Middle Ages the sin of simony.

Cook: It may not sound like the biggest deal today to us, but obviously it was such an important thing in Dante's day. In fact, by 1300, the Church had been campaigning for 200 years against the buying and selling of church offices, but, in fact, not only had it probably gotten worse, but it had, if you will, trickled up so that the popes themselves were involved, and, in fact, we're going to be—in the 19th canto—in the third ditch of the eighth circle, where we have popes who are being punished for this sin. So, it's a very serious sin in Dante's day. A second thing that makes this canto important for the dynamic of the Inferno is, we're going, really, to see here the growth of Dante the pilgrim. That is to say, obviously, if we take the whole hundred cantos, to use Ron's phrase from an earlier lecture, Dante starts out dumb and ends up smart, In some ways the 19th canto is that movement in microcosm, and therefore, even in the course of 140 or so lines, the average length of a cantos, we're going to see real change in the character of Dante the pilgrim.

Herzman: One other thing to say before we find our way into the text, we've been talking in various places about the kind of audacity of Dante to write a poem like this, a poem of this magnitude, a poem that takes on these subjects, but this is sort of a good place to see the audacity of his presuming to know what people's final resting place in the afterlife is going to be, because, of course, he doesn't hesitate to put in this particular cantos, this *bolgia*, popes, the spiritual leaders of Christendom in his time, and it seems to me that we have to kind of remind ourselves of just how radical such an assessment would have been, and just how sort of fraught with danger, almost, Dante's decision to do that would be seen as. It's very interesting to think about this also as a kind of microcosm of Dante's audacity in writing the entire *Commedia*.

Cook: We begin with Dante the poet, the author of this poem, really strongly speaking to us and sort of waving a flag in our faces saying "Pay attention folks, this is a big one."

> O Simon Magus! O scum that followed him!
>   Those things of God that rightly should be wed
>   to holiness, you, rapacious creatures,
>
> for the price of gold and silver, prostitute.

Well, he begins with a particular name, Simon Magus. It turns out to be a character, oddly enough, in the Bible; in particular in the Acts of the Apostles he makes a fairly brief appearance. Peter and John are laying on hands and conveying the Holy Spirit, and Simon comes along in Chapter 8 of Acts and says, "That's really cool. I would really like to do that. How much does it cost?" Peter has an interesting response; I paraphrase but not very much, "Go to hell, Simon. Go to Perdition. The things you're talking about are things of the spirit, and you can't use money to purchase things of the spirit. You're really radically confused." So, this biblical character is invoked here in the very beginning.

Herzman: It turns out that this biblical character also has a kind of interesting post-biblical life. Not being satisfied with Peter's answer, he goes out and learns the arts of Black Magic, and then comes back to kind of bug Peter, that's the technical word. What he actually does is spend a lot of time kind of opposing Peter, his magic versus

Peter's teaching and healing, and it all comes to this great climax in this sort of Western shootout before the letter, when they get to Rome and Simon goes up to the gates of Rome, jumps off, and begins flying around and basically says, "Hey everyone, look at me. Who do you want to follow? That guy down there or me?" Peter prays and says, "Lord, if this keeps going an awful lot of people are going to go over to Simon," and at that point he does this wonderful nose-dive, hits the ground, and sort of goes into the ground so that his feet are kind of flapping in the breeze, and this image of the fall of Simon the Magician, *magus* is simply the Latin word for magician, becomes a very popular image throughout the Middle Ages, and especially from the 12th century on, to depict kind of the consequences of this sin of simony. So, followers of Simon are simoniacs. They buy and they sell church offices. That is to say, more generally, they kind of take the things of the spirit and pervert them for their own material gain. So, in this ringing invocation at the beginning, the poet is saying "Pay attention; this is a biggie, and I'm going to give you a real treat in terms of what I'm doing here."

Cook: So, after this invocation, Dante and Virgil begin to explore what's going on here. They sort of look around and see what they see, and what that is is stone holes, holes cut in the stone at the bottom of this ditch, and there are legs sticking out and flapping around and whatever, and in the description of that, as Dante so often does, he says, "Let me tell you what that sort of reminded me of, let me give you an earthly analog."

> To me they (the holes) seemed no wider and no deeper
> than those inside my lovely San Giovanni,
> in which the priest would stand or baptize from;
>
> and one of these, not so many years ago,
> I smashed for someone who was drowning in it:
> let this be mankind's picture of the truth!

Well, let's start with just unpacking the image. There was a separate building for baptism because baptism was a communal event in Italy in the Middle Ages, and therefore the Baptistery of Florence was in a real sense the center of town, and if you went inside in the Middle Ages—alas not now because the furnishings have changed, but there are furnishings like these that survive in other places such as Pisa—you would have found a baptismal font, sort of a hexagonal pond, and you would have had stone holes at each one of those corners big enough for somebody to stand in, and therefore what you'd have is, on the day of the year when all of the babies were baptized who were born that previous year, the priest would stand in those holes, take the baby from somebody, turn around, baptize the baby in the water, and then turn around and hand the baby back, and he said, "Those stone holes down in hell reminded me of these, and by the way," he says, "I took a sledgehammer one day and smashed that sucker in the Baptistery of Florence," presumably because something like this had happened. "When it wasn't in use, one of those holes had gotten some water in it, and a baby had gotten stuck in it and was in danger of drowning, so I smashed the baptismal font to save a baby from death." It seemed like an odd incident, that Dante sort of justified something he did back on earth, but also there's no historical record it ever happened. We don't know for sure. But, at any rate, it just sort of adds to the fact we have to ask what is Dante doing here in this little apparent aside?

Herzman: Well, one of the things that he seems to be doing is apologizing for something that, if misunderstood, if seen from the outside, would seem like an act of blasphemy. That is to say, here he is going around with a sledgehammer, destroying church property, and you can just see the tabloids, "Dante—Local Poet Turns Out To Be Church Destroyer" and there's a little picture of Dante with his hammer. What he's saying is, of course, that wasn't the picture at all. What I was doing was saving someone's life. So, it seems to us that what he's really trying to say is, by analogy, folks are going to say exactly the same thing about what is going on in this cantos. That is to say, it looks like I'm smashing church property, metaphorically, because what I'm doing is criticizing in the most serious possible way the abuses that are committed by churchmen at the time, starting with the top. Here's what our spiritual leaders have done. Well, again, the superficial way of responding to that would be to say, "Blasphemy, blasphemy, look at what Dante is doing," but he's sort of asking us to think by analogy with what he does to the baptismal font, and say, "What I was trying to do was to bring life and to do that I had to smash a little property." Here what he is trying to do in the cantos as a whole, and we would even argue in the *Commedia* as a whole, is bring life to a moribund church. A church that is more concerned with wealth and property, with material things, than it is with its spiritual mission. Indeed, the whole point of using that Simon the Magician analogy is to talk about how the relationship between the spiritual and the material has been totally turned upside down. So he's saying, "Here I am to try to get things right. People aren't going to like it very much. People are going to misinterpret it, but nonetheless, here it is, deal with it."

Cook: So here with pen rather than hammer Dante is going to take on the same job, and as he now continues the description what he sees is that these holes at the bottom of this ditch in hell are filled, and they're filled with legs. That is to say, people are in them upside down and their legs are flapping, and on top of the feet that are flapping are, in fact, flames. This is a very important image, because the so-called birthday of the Church is the Feast of Pentecost, the descent of the Holy Spirit, which comes as tongues of flame on the heads of the Apostles. Well, of course, the pope is the successor of the Apostle Peter in particular, and so what we have here is how upside down simony makes everything, because these guys are upside down and this is flame, and this is flame that hurts, by the way. There is flame on their feet. They really are literally upside down. They are perversions of the gift of the Holy Spirit by seeing these feet flapping and fiery.

Herzman: Now, they're down in the ditch. Dante is with Virgil, and Virgil says, "You better go down there to figure out what's going on." Dante doesn't—at this point, the pilgrim—know who's there. He says,

> 'Whatever you are, holding your upside down,
>> O wretched soul, stuck like a stake in the ground,
>> make a sound or something,' [I said,] 'if you can.'

So, he sort of walks down there. You can imagine the scene. He's standing, legs sticking out, flaming legs of all things, and he says,

> I stood there like a priest who is confessing
>> some vile assassin who, fixed in his ditch,
>> has called him back again to put off dying.

This, too, is a kind of contemporary reference.

Cook: It's a really neat one because we know that the penalty in Florence for being what we would call a hired gun or a hired assassin was to be buried alive upside down. They would dig a hole, lower the body in headfirst; then, before they filled in the dirt, a priest would come to hear the last confession for the good of the soul of the assassin. So, Dante says, "I'm there like," keep in mind that there is a pope down there, "but I'm there like the priest hearing the confession of an assassin." In fact, Dante is here playing that role of hearing the confession of the pope, and the pope is a kind of assassin. He really is, in some way, an assassin of the Church by the way that this pope and others like him, as it turns out, are involved in the buying and selling of church offices.

Herzman: That vile assassin begins to speak. Remember, the date is 1300. The pope who is alive and reigning back on earth is Boniface VIII, and it's sort of interesting then to see what this speaker, this pope, this upside-down successor of Simon Magus rather than successor of the first pope, Simon Peter, he says to Dante, "'Is that you here already upright? / Is that you here already upright, Boniface?'" In other words, what he had done, he has mistaken Dante for Boniface because he hears that Boniface is going to come down and be his successor.

> 'Are you fed up so soon with all that wealth
> for which you did not fear to take by guile
> the Lovely Lady, (That is to say the Church, of course) then tear her asunder?'

So, here we have this wonderful kind of comedy of errors where one pope is accusing Dante of being another who has done even worse things than he has. That he's saying, essentially, "I was pretty good at this simony stuff, but compared to you I'm just playing minor league ball. You're in the majors." Of course, Dante is saying, "What's going on here? What's going on?" Well, the poet, of course, knows exactly what's going on.

Cook: But, Dante the pilgrim, just for a while, just can't answer. I mean, it's such an absurd question. You know, here's this guy, and he's being asked the question, "Aren't you Pope Boniface VIII?" It's like saying to Ron, "Aren't you Lawrence of Arabia?" That is such an absurd question that you stop and say, "Now, there must be something beyond the obvious as to what that question means because it is such a dumb question." So Dante sort of stammers for a little bit and Virgil has to say, "Just tell him you're not Boniface VIII," and Dante's finally able to get that out and solve this little problem.

I want you to notice, though, that what Dante's done here is really ingenious because, as we've said several times, rule number one of the game for being in the Inferno is that you've got to be dead by 1300, but Boniface, in fact, doesn't die until 1303, that's after Dante is writing, the date where the poem is set but before Dante writes the poem. So this is a way for Dante to be able to discuss Boniface VIII directly in hell even though he isn't there yet as it turns out.

Herzman: So, he gets Boniface in hell by anticipation, and, you know, I say "What's going on here?" Of course, when really it is the poet himself who makes sure that we know what Boniface's final resting place is going to be. We still don't know, however, who the person is who's talking. That identification comes just a little bit later. So, to the spirit then, Dante answers, "No, no—I'm not he, I'm not he."

> The spirit heard, and twisted both his feet,…
>   'Well, then, what do you want of me?
>
> If it concerns you so to learn my name
>   that for this reason you came down the bank,
>   know that I was once dressed in the great mantle.

A kind of fancy way of saying, "I was once pope."

> But actually I was the she-bear's son,
>   so greedy to advance my cubs, that wealth
>   I pocketed in life, and here, myself.'

Well, this passage too deserves a little unpacking.

Cook: First of all, when he says I was the son of the she-bear, he's identifying his family name because he comes from a Roman family named "Orsini" and from that we know who he is, Pope Nicholas III. Pope Nicholas III was a member of the Orsini family, and he was pope about 20 years before this poem was set. He died, in fact, in 1280. But keep in mind this, when someone becomes pope, let's say the current pope—John Paul II—he takes a new name. You don't become Pope Karol Wojtyla, you become Pope John Paul II, and there's a long tradition in both the Old and New Testaments of a new name referring to a new identity, a new meaning, a new job to do. So, Abram becomes Abraham, and Saul becomes Paul, and so what we're told is that popes do the same thing. They leave aside. They put behind family, as they come to be called to govern the universal

Church. But notice what he says, that I've put on "the great mantle," but I actually remained the she-bear's son. I remained an Orsini. I was operating as pope as an Orsini. I was wheeling and dealing for the Orsini family. I was taking all the cousins and giving them church offices because I was setting up the Orsini family for a long time in the future to remain powerful, and, of course, in saying this I really remained the "son of the she-bear." He's also telling us exactly why he is guilty of the sin of simony.

Herzman: Notice also at the last part of that tercet, "that wealth I pocketed in life," okay, getting rich from the Church, and here pocketed myself. In other words, the punishment is to be in these pockets, these upside-down holes, so you have another wonderful example of the punishment reenacting the crime, the punishment being the crime, the punishment fitting the crime. So, essentially, this kind of pocketing, this upside-down pocketing is the greed; this is the greed reenacted that he did before. Now, notice one of the things that is kind of nifty here about the positioning. Remember, Dante is like the friar hearing the confession, and the pope here, Nicholas, is like the assassin. Well, this is like a confession. Dante is there listening to this catalog of sins of this sort of nepotism and greed on the part of Nicholas III. Well, the thing that is kind of nifty about it is that, once again, it's a kind of parody of confession. It's not the real thing, it's the letter without the spirit, not simply because Dante is not really a priest, but most of all because Nicholas isn't really sorry for what he's doing. This is confession without sorrow or repentance. In fact, it kind of feels like he's bragging about what he did. He lists all of these things and then says, "There's a long list of people who are going to be guilty of this kind of hanky-panky."

Cook: "Let me tell you how this is set up," he says,

> 'Beneath my head are pushed down all the others
>   who came, sinning in simony, before me,
>   squeezed tightly in the fissure of the rock.'

Then he goes on to say, "When Boniface comes, I'm going to be squeezed down." So there's a succession of folks that are in the rock, and only one is flapping his legs at any given time, the others are pushed down further and further and further in the rock. Now, go back to what we started with at the beginning of this lecture, and go back to the first line of this canto, "Oh Simon Magus and the story we told." You can see how these are really the guys who are the followers of Simon Magus. They are in the succession of Simon Magus. The problem is they are supposed to be in the succession of Saint Peter. They are, after all, as popes, the followers of Peter, whose, by the way, name is Simon; Simon Bar Jonah is Peter's name. So, they have followed the wrong Simon. Instead of being those who were on the rock, because "on this rock, Peter, I will found my Church," they are the successors of Simon Magus, who is in the rock.

Herzman: Notice that up until this point we have, actually ourselves, made the point that whenever the pilgrim hears somebody's story, his general tendency is to sympathize with them, to kind of become involved, as he was with Francesca, let's say, or the pity he feels for Pier delle Vigne. But here he has an altogether different response, and for the first time we sort of see the pilgrim draw back and become extremely critical, even sarcastic and nasty, to Nicholas. A very proper reaction to it, we might add, because he seems so fed up with this recollection, this reflection on just how corrupt the papacy has become.

> I do not know, perhaps I was too bold here,
>> but I answered him in tune with his own words:
>> 'Well, tell me now: what was the sum of money
>
> that holy Peter had to pay our Lord
>> before He gave the keys into his keeping?
>> Certainly He asked no more than 'Follow me.'
>
> Nor did Peter or the rest extort gold coins
>> or silver from Matthias when he was picked
>> to fill the place the evil one had lost.'

Cook: This is one of several references in this canto to the Acts of the Apostles. We've already suggested that Simon Magus himself is a character in the Acts of the Apostles. The Feast of the Pentecost is described in the Acts of the Apostles. This is a reference to the first story in the Acts of the Apostles, how do we replace Judas? Remember what Judas's sin was, and the 40 pieces of silver, 30 pieces of silver, and all that sort of stuff. How do we replace Judas? Well, as Dante is saying to those feet down there, "Peter didn't say, 'Whose going to bid the most for this job?' right?" Of course not, it was done, as we learned in Acts, by lots so there would be no hanky-panky, if you will. That God, therefore, would choose a successor of

Judas. So, going back to that great text, the Acts of the Apostles, the story of the early Church, Dante is invoking a number of images here, and really sort of pointing his finger, really letting Nicholas III have it.

Herzman: In fact, he keeps going as though he himself is sort of building up to this great crescendo.

> 'And were it not for the reverence I have
> > for those highest of all keys that you once held
> > in the happy life—if this did not restrain me,

(it doesn't sound all that restrained to me)

> I would use even harsher words than these,
> > for your avarice brings grief upon the world,
> > crushing the good, exhausting the depraved.'

In fact, it might be worth saying just a word or two of just what the consequences are of this sort of ecclesiastical hanky-panky and see how it's something that's not just a matter of Church business, and Church corruption as such.

Why, after all, would you buy an office? Well, presumably because it's an investment. Presumably you would buy an office so that you can make a profit. So, why would somebody buy an office from, say, a pope? Say, a bishop? Well, because the bishop can make a profit, make a profit on the wealth that the Church owns, make a profit, perhaps, in allotting the lesser jobs in the bishop's court or even the offices of parish priest. So, it really is trickle-down corruption. But there's another problem—who's going to become bishop if there's a price tag? And, of course, one answer is nobody who should be a bishop, because a) people who should be bishops and priests won't have lots of bucks and b) if they did, they wouldn't buy offices because they know that is against God's teaching. So, it ruins the entire structure of the Church. It exalts the wrong folks, and the folks that need to hold those offices are absolutely excluded. From top to bottom, the Church's ruin begins here, in the way he tells the story, with papal corruption.

Herzman: Of course, notice also that what it means is that particular popes—let's take Boniface VIII, for example. Boniface VIII has access to resources—monetary and financial—that he otherwise wouldn't and couldn't have, and those resources are precisely what enables him, well ultimately, to kick Dante and the White Guelfs out of Florence. So, there's that connection also. All of this stuff isn't just *cosa nostra*, it's not just the Church and its own business; it's the way the Church impacts on society as a whole as well.

Cook: Dante, notice in this speech, also says, by the way, "stay stuck there, for you are rightly punished." We want to sort of throw up our hands for the first time and say, "Dante, you hear, understand what God is doing, and you're siding with God. You are finally seeing what the gate of hell says in Inferno 3. This is a place of justice; this seems to be the first time when Dante really perceives the justice of the place. Stay right where you are, and Dante is sort of saying, "I accept the fact that God's got this exactly right."

Herzman: It's interesting to see how the pilgrim himself builds up to a kind of rhetorical climax here. He's still going on and he says,

> 'You have built yourself a God of gold and silver!
>   How do you differ from the idolater,
>   except he worships one, you worship hundreds?'

That is to say the worship of the gold and the silver, which, of course, is what introduced the canto in the first place.

Well, what's kind of nifty about that, in fact, there's a line from Saint Paul, who sort of equates avarice with idolatry, and Dante the poet is sort of picking up on that here to talk about the way in which the worst of all sins, the sort of first commandment being broken here, is really what these popes are all about. But then he hits his climax at the end.

> 'O Constantine, what evil did you sire,
>   not by your conversion, but by the dower
>   that the first wealthy father got from you.'

Again, on a line that deserves some unpacking. He's talking here about Constantine the Emperor; what's he doing here? What's the point of that?

Cook: A thousand years ago, Constantine became a Christian, the first Christian emperor from which there are enormous consequences, and a popular medieval story, which wasn't debunked until the 15th century—after Dante's time—says that when Constantine moved from Rome to his new city, named for his favorite person—Constantinople—that is to say, what he did was give a lot of wealth and even political power to the Bishop of Rome, that is to say, to the pope. "So Constantine," Dante says, "what did you start here? You gave wealth to the Church, and now look what's happened. A real condemnation that's now a thousand years old." But what's interesting is, Constantine is somebody we're going to meet up with in the afterlife. Dante has placed him in the afterlife. Constantine is in heaven, because although Constantine did this thing with awful consequences, as it turns out, he meant well. He meant to support and sustain a new Church that was just emerging from the time of persecution, and it was probably not possible for him to see the damage that would be caused a long time in the future. So, he becomes one of the interesting figures we'll watch for in Paradise.

Herzman: Now, notice there are a couple of things going on here. First, just in terms of Dante's whole system, it is very important to remind ourselves that people are punished or rewarded because of their motivation. So, as Bill pointed out, Constantine meant well, and is rewarded for that. So it is important to keep that in mind. It's also important to see in sort of giving us this final ringing peroration here, "O Constantine, what evil did you sire?" that the pilgrim sounds suspiciously like the poet did in the opening, "O Simon Magus." That was the poet speaking, kind of warning his audience, "Hey, we're going to get to something really good now." At the end, the pilgrim's knowledge has reached that of the poet, and we see in that what Dante has learned in this canto.

Cook: From here, we're going to continue to look at the eighth circle by meeting two very interesting sinners, a little bit further down, in the next lecture.

Lecture Ten
The False Counselors

Scope:

This lecture continues the discussion of fraud by examining a sin that is often called by critics "false counsel." In Canto 26, we meet an ancient practitioner of this sin in the figure of Ulysses. In Canto 27, we meet a figure from Dante's own time, Guido da Montefeltro, a soldier turned Franciscan friar. For Ulysses, Dante creates a "sequel" to his famous story by sending him on another journey after his return home from Troy. This journey reveals his sin. With Guido, Dante encounters a modern example of the same sin in a figure who "repents" but then takes up his old ways again at the urging of Boniface VIII in an audacious but failed attempt to defraud God. Through these two complementary figures, we learn about the perversion of the intellect that is fraud.

Outline

I. The sin often called "false counsel" is punished in the eighth *bolgia* of the eighth circle.

   A. The circle is described in two cantos.

   B. Each canto presents a dramatic encounter with a practitioner of this kind of deceit, encased in a tongue of flame that vibrates when the damned soul "speaks."

   C. Canto 26 is the story of the great classical figure Ulysses, whom Dante knows only from Latin sources, including summaries of Homer's *Odyssey.* Dante discusses Ulysses as he appears in the *Aeneid,* then adds to that story.

   D. Canto 27 is the story of Guido da Montefeltro, a modern example.

   E. The two figures, classic and contemporary, are in many ways complementary and help the reader focus on the nature of the sin.

   1. Each has a kind of superior intelligence.

   2. Each is able to attract followers.

II. The first false counselor is Ulysses, whom we meet in Inferno 26.

    A. He is encased in a tongue of flame.

    B. He is in the eighth *bolgia* with another classical figure, Diomede, who was his partner in crime.

    C. We are told of their earlier crimes, which Dante takes from various classical sources.

III. Then Ulysses tells the story of his adventures after he has come home from Troy.

    A. This part of his narrative is Dante's own invention, a sequel to the story of Odysseus's homecoming in the *Odyssey* (which Dante did not know directly).

    B. Ulysses directly inverts the virtue of *pietas* through his failure to be loyal to father, son, and wife.

    C. He is an anti-Aeneas, negating the great qualities of loyalty and commitment to virtue that Aeneas models.

    D. What is important for Ulysses is adventure simply for its own sake, an ideal of "heroic discovery" detached from any other set of values or obligations and, hence, morally obtuse at best and vicious at worst.

    E. He leads his men to death, with no heed to their own capabilities or needs.

    F. He abandons not only family but the kingdom he is charged with ruling; his wayward hunger for new experiences has significant and evil social consequences.

    G. Ulysses was often seen in romantic readings of the poem as a heroic figure, but as a false journeyer, a false pilgrim, he is rather a negative example for Dante.

        1. Dante needs to learn to see his own journey as fundamentally different from that of Ulysses.

        2. Dante must recognize that his own temptations are the temptations that come from talent, ability, and superior intelligence.

        3. Ulysses's call for his men to trust him is ironic in view of his own refusal to take things "on trust" (i.e., without seeing for himself).

IV. Guido da Montefeltro provides a contemporary story of "false counsel," parallel in many ways to that of Ulysses.

A. He is famed as a military tactician, sort of a medieval version of a "think tank" strategist.

B. He tells Dante the story of his conversion to the religious life as a Franciscan brother.

    1. The reader is left to wonder whether the conversion was sincere or was simply his attempt to trick God.

    2. His own language and his subsequent story strongly suggest the latter.

C. He continues the story by telling how he was "tricked" away from his religious life and brought back to his old ways by Pope Boniface VIII.

    1. He accepts an offer of forgiveness in advance of the sin.

    2. He claims it was an offer he couldn't refuse.

    3. But it is clear that the offer itself was a sham and a contradiction in terms.

    4. The poet makes some key points about the nature of repentance.

    5. He also takes another opportunity to criticize Boniface VIII.

D. Like other sinners in hell, Guido is trying to place the blame on someone else, in his case, Pope Boniface.

E. However, he is a betrayer who is himself betrayed.

V. Guido and Ulysses taken together serve as powerful examples of the nature of fraud and of the evil it works on communities.

Readings:

Inferno, Cantos 20–27.

Virgil, *The Aeneid of Virgil*, Book 2.

Questions to Consider:

1. Why does Dante create this fantastic ending to the life of Ulysses given that so much material is available for him to use in his encounter with the sinner?

2. What should we call the sin that Ulysses and Guido are being punished for?

3. What lesson do we learn about those who deceive others?

Lecture Ten—Transcript
The False Counselors

Cook: Remember that we left off in the eighth circle. Ron pointed out in the last lecture that there are, in fact, two circles of fraud, circles eight and nine. We're in the area of what's called "simple fraud" as opposed to "compound fraud." Compound fraud, the ninth circle—we'll be dealing with that in the next lecture—is fraud perpetrated against those for whom there is a special bond of trust, and so we're going to remain now in the eighth circle where we have this simple fraud, and we've already seen that wonderful event where Dante sort of gets God's justice in his conversation with Nicholas III. We've got to tell you, it's a rocky road. Even when Dante makes progress, it's not automatically downhill—literally or any other way—from here on. For example, in the very next canto, where Dante encounters fortunetellers, their punishment involves such twisted bodies, or shapes technically, that Dante starts weeping, and Virgil really lets him have it and says, "You know, stop that. This is not a place for that." Dante has been a backslider in a certain way. It reminds us that although Dante in some ways is over a particular intellectual hump when he has this encounter with Nicholas III, it's by no means automatic. It's not a habit yet, and we're going to see a lot of backsliding on Dante's part. He's still got a lot to learn. We still have four-fifths of the poem to go.

We're going to focus now, for the rest of this lecture, in a particular ditch of this eighth circle, where unusually for the *Divine Comedy* Dante and Virgil have two totally different conversations in the same place with different people. So, it's going to be a way where we're going to have two very different looks at the same sin, which will allow us to stop at the end and say, "'What exactly is the nature of this sin?" It doesn't have as obvious a label, as obvious a name, as simony or pandering or seducing, or flattering or fortune telling or whatever. So, we're going to be looking at Cantos 26 and 27. Virgil primarily chatting with Ulysses, and then Dante chatting with a more or less contemporary Italian named Guido da Montefeltro.

Herzman: Whatever the sin is called, it's a sin of misdirected intellect, and the two figures represent that with an ancient model, Ulysses and the more modern model. Let's talk a little bit about Ulysses first. Dante certainly knew about Ulysses, but he only knew about Ulysses from the Latin sources, not originally from the Greek, so that for example, the heroic Odysseus, the hero of Homer's great epic, Dante doesn't know about him first-hand, only in summaries that had been handed down to him in Latin translation, but he knew the role that Odysseus, now become Ulysses, had in Virgil's *Aeneid*, and basically his role there was to be resident slime-ball among the Greeks. In fact, one of the things that is very interesting about Dante's portrayal of Ulysses here is that he starts out taking the Ulysses that is present in the *Aeneid*, giving us a picture of that guy, but then extending the story. That is to say, Dante's own creation becomes part of this canto where he takes what's known and adds to it his own version of the story. It turns out that they have a really interesting punishment, these sinners; they are encased in a tongue of flame. All right, they're sort of inside flames, and when Virgil and Dante encounter this sort of split flame, we find out that it has inside it Ulysses and his buddy Diomed, that is to say, the guy who was his buddy in perpetrating all kinds of fraudulent things in Virgil's *Aeneid*. So, essentially what you get is that Ulysses.

> He said: 'Within Ulysses and Diomed
> are suffering in anger with each other,
> just vengeance makes them march together now.'

They are one of the pairs that Dante the poet seems to be so interested in. We had Francesca and Paolo, we had Farinata and Cavalcante, and now we have Ulysses and Diomed, and he says, "All right, there."

> 'And they lament inside one flame the ambush
> of the horse become the gateway that allowed
> the Romans' noble seed to issue forth.'

In other words, that's a reference to Book II of the *Aeneid*, which we spoke of earlier. The fall of Troy. Ulysses was the great engineer of the Trojan horse. He is the one who's responsible for that stratagem, and for that he's being punished now, and also being punished for the theft of the Palladium. Again, Book II of the *Aeneid* steals a statue of Minerva, again a kind of sacrilege. In Virgil's poem that's what he's here for. But it turns out that what he did in the past becomes somewhat less significant to Dante than what happened after that in a story that he tells to Virgil about what happens after he gets back from the Trojan War.

Cook: Remember how it basically goes, 10 years in the Trojan War, 10 years getting back to Ithaca—where he's from, where he's left dad, his wife, and his son. So, you may recall if you've done the Homeric version this great homecoming scene. Well, this is very much redone here; again, as Ron pointed out, Dante had not read Homer. What we're told is when he gets home,

> 'not sweetness of the son, not reverence
> for an aging father, not the debt of love
> I owed Penelope to make her happy,
>
> could quench deep in myself the burning wish
> to know the world and have experience
> of all man's vices, of all human worth.'

He gets home, hangs his hat up, and says, "Gosh, haven't done everything, haven't been everywhere, bye," and takes a journey. Now, you might ask, what's Dante's source for this? I don't recall this either in the *Aeneid* or in the *Odyssey*; where does Dante get this? And as far as scholars know, and God knows they've searched a lot, Dante makes it up. That is to say, this is one of the great creative moments where Dante takes this age-old story and he adds to it and carries it out, in fact, to the death of Odysseus.

Herzman: I might add that Dante's willingness to do this is one sign among many that Dante gives to his readers that I want to play with the really big boys, that regarding the unsurpassed reputation of Homer, and the reality as well as the reputation of Virgil. Dante says, "Well, okay, I'm going to add something to it myself from that story, that Trojan story, that's new and that's original and that takes things in a rather different way." Notice also, by the way, that coming home to wife and to father and to son is a very good thing to do, but even more the virtues of loyalty to family as represented in wife and son and father would have been pretty much what would have defined another hero that Dante is constantly bringing up, Aeneas himself. In other words, what we're seeing here is that the way to take a look at Ulysses as Dante describes him is as kind of an anti-Aeneas. Here are the qualities that he had as a hero. Ulysses is the guy who negates all of those qualities by saying that kind of loyalty, that kind of pull, that kind of tie, that doesn't count anymore. What I want to do is to go out there and to have experience, and experience, as he puts it, all of man's vices, all human worth, and we have to ask ourselves whether or not in fact experiencing human vices is a good thing to do. It seems to me that you could argue that if it's—let's say your thing is you're very interested in the drug problem and you want to deal with rehabilitation, it makes a lot of sense to visit a lot of rehab clinics and do all of that kind of stuff. It doesn't make sense to say, well, in order to understand this from the inside, I think what I will do is shoot a lot of cocaine and a lot of heroin because that way I'll be able to understand what goes on much better, that there's a kind of knowledge that it is better off for us not to have, and the most important thing I think that is coming out of this canto is that we have to learn how it is that we're able to make distinctions between knowledge that's worth having and worth going after, and knowledge that is forbidden. Essentially, Ulysses's T-shirt reads "No Knowledge Is Forbidden," no such thing as forbidden knowledge, and it seems to me that that is the portrait that Dante is having Ulysses paint for himself.

Cook: It's also ultimately we all know, just not in the cards to be able to experience everything. For example, this is something that Augustine had to learn. I can't experience everything. Sooner or later I have to decide what I trust, and whom I trust, and, of course, Ulysses trusts only his own experiences, in particular he trusts only his own sense perception, and he talks about the fact that, "If I can't perceive it with the senses, then I have no access to it and I want to know everything, and so I've got to experience with my senses everything." There's another important facet as he takes off on this journey; he doesn't do it alone. It isn't that I'm going to put on my backpack and go out and learn everything, it's he fires up the old boat and the sailors who came back with him, and they all take off together. Dante said, "These are tired men. These are men like Ulysses who've been away for many, many years, but he is the King, after all, of Ithaca, and so there is an enormous social consequence to this that sounds like a kind of solitary request for experience, and we never want to lose track of the fact that whatever happens to Ulysses happens to a lot of other folks in this journey as well.

Herzman: In fact, one of the things that Ulysses is good at—in Homer's version, in Virgil's version, here in Dante's version—is giving a good speech. He's doing that to Virgil, of course, down in hell, but what he does is sort of recreate the speech that he gives to these tired old men to get them to go on the journey with him.

> 'Brothers,' I [Dante] said, 'who though a hundred thousand
>   perils have made your way to reach the West,
>   during this so brief vigil of our senses

...do not deny
　　yourself experience of what is there beyond,
　　behind the sun, in the world they call unpeopled.'

Well, by the time he finished the speech, as they say in the coaching biz, they're ready to run through a wall for him, and they do, and essentially the pitch that he's giving to them is, "Hey, trust me." In fact, that trust leads nowhere except to their death, and it's also interesting to see—he has this wonderful image talking about what they're doing. "We made our oars our wings for that mad flight." Well, of course, the people who are imagining the oars are these old guys that he has gotten to go along with him. So, there's a sense in which the fraud that we're dealing with is the ability of somebody to persuade others to do things for you. That seems to be a large part of what Ulysses here is all about.

Cook: Notice, as Ron so well put it, he's saying to these guys, "Trust me." This is a guy who doesn't trust anybody. This is the guy who says I've got to do it all, see it all, touch it all, smell it all, myself. This is the guy who won't buy anybody else's version but he's saying to them: "Trust me." Again, what a wonderful way of thinking about what fraud is. Here's a guy that says "Trust me, I don't' trust anything."

Herzman: What's sort of interesting is that their symbol for going beyond the limits of already-understood knowledge was to go outside the straights of Gibraltar, and they sail out there. Now, we mentioned in an earlier lecture that nobody in Dante's time thought the earth was flat. The only people who really thought the world was flat were the people who made up the history books in the 1950s. They knew the earth was round, but what they weren't quite sure of was the exact size, and they tended to get it a little bit smaller, and because of that, of course—this relates to Columbus a little bit later on—they didn't believe that there was a large land mass between where they knew that they were, and the east. So, Columbus, he tried to make the voyage to the east, and ran into the Americas instead. Ulysses, he gets out there, and what he runs into is the most wonderful, one of the most wonderful, of Dante's creations—Mount Purgatory—which is, in fact, what we're going to be talking about when we deal with purgatory in subsequent lectures. He gets there from a distance; he sees it, and all of a sudden the ship sinks. What's important, of course, is he leads himself and his men to death, but also it turns out that this is a kind of nifty image for the fact that Ulysses is a kind of model for Dante's pilgrimage, and it tells us that Dante is doing it the right way, with Virgil as his guide; remember what Bill said about Ulysses's "do it myself" attitude. What Dante gets to with the guidance of Virgil and the help that comes to him ultimately from above, Ulysses is trying to do on his own. Ulysses doesn't get to seize the mountain, falls, and dies, but, of course, in the process leads a lot of other people to death with him.

> '...three times in churning waters;
> > the fourth blast raised the stern up high, and sent
> > the bow down deep, as pleased Another's will.

> And then the sea was closed again, above us.'

And we see the ending of Ulysses and his men.

Cook: In the next canto, again Dante and Virgil stay in the same place, in the same *bolgia*. And therefore they meet up with another sinner, that is to say, incased in a flame. But it's a very different conversation. Virgil really does the talking with Ulysses. Now, Dante will do the talking with, again, roughly an older contemporary Guido da Montefeltro, who had been dead a very short time in 1300, and therefore if we don't have a label right away for what exactly the specific sin of Ulysses is within that category of fraud, perhaps we'll be able to figure out what the nature of this is by looking at another example of it and sort of playing the oldest game in the world—take two different stories and see what they have in common. What is it that's going to link these two very different stories in terms of the essence of what these sinners tell us about themselves? Guido da Montefeltro was a nobleman from the northern part of Italy. He was a political partisan. He was a Ghibelline leader for many years, and right at the end of his life he decided he would become something else. He became a member of the Franciscan Order, and, in fact, he gets involved in some of the political shenanigans of Pope Boniface VIII. So, his story is going to relate to some of the other stories we've heard, especially, for example, the story of Boniface VIII by anticipation in Inferno 19, and I think we'll find this is one of the most interesting and very deep parts of the entire Inferno.

Herzman: Notice also in terms of what Bill said before about what connects the two. One thing that strikes me know, just as Bill says this, is clearly Guido's story is implicated in all of the events of

Dante's own life since it deals with Boniface VIII and all the political stuff that clearly results in Dante's own exile. So, what you have is a story that is obviously related to Dante, and therefore had a kind of direct relevance and a direct message for him, but it is important to point out that exactly the same thing is true with the Ulysses story earlier, which is to say, what Ulysses's tendency to do is say, "Look, I have the kind of talent and ability that allows me to manipulate, that allows me to get what I want, and that creates a huge temptation," a temptation that Ulysses obviously gives into quite readily. For Dante, he has to see that there's a kind of similar temptation in his journey, if you will, because, of course, for Dante he's got to recognize that he has, himself, a kind of talent and ability, and the question is, how to put that to use? So, the story of Ulysses's journey really becomes a lightening rod for all of the concerns of Dante the pilgrim in this broad metaphorical way as Guido da Montefeltro's story becomes a lightening rod for Dante in a very precise and clearly specific way.

Cook: Let's take a look at how Guido introduces himself by telling a little bit of his own story. He says,

> 'I was a man of arms and then a friar,
>> believing with the cord to make amends;
>> and surely my belief would have come true
>
> were it not for that High Priest [read Boniface] (his soul be damned!)
>> who put me back among my early sins;
>> I want to tell you why and how it happened.
>
> While I still had the form of bones and flesh
>> my mother gave me, all my actions were
>> not those of a lion, but those of a fox;
>
> the wiles and covert paths, I knew them all,
>> and so employed my art that rumor of me
>> spread to the farthest limits of the earth.'

First of all, that is probably not true, by the way, he's a fairly important regional figure, hardly a worldwide figure, but notice he uses this image of the lion and the fox. "I was tricky. I didn't win battles by being the strongest guy on the battlefield. I knew how to do all the diplomatic parts, I knew how to out-fox," we would say today, "my opponents. I could beat guys stronger than me because I was really, really clever." So this is the kind of military career that Guido had. Well, then, why abandon it and become a Franciscan?

Herzman: The first thing I want to say is that that description that Bill just gave sounds an awful lot like Ulysses. The second thing is, he abandoned it because—he says,

> 'When I saw that the time of life had come
> for me, as it must come for every man
> to lower the sails and gather in the lines,'

Notice, by the way, that what he's doing there is saying, "Here we are getting close to the end, and I've got to sort of think about my soul now." But he uses the metaphor of life as a sea voyage, which, of course, is another neat linkage to Ulysses, but then he says, All right,

> 'things I once found pleasure in then grieved me;
> repentant and confessed, I took the vows
> a monk takes. And...

(then, in one of the great lines that anybody speaks, I think, to Dante)

> ... oh, to think it could have worked!'

There are a couple of ways to take a look at that. One of them is to assume yes, he really was repentant, and that would have worked and he would have been saved except that he went back to his old ways. This story that he is telling is in parts here, but it seems to us, at any rate, that it makes a whole lot more sense to read this as, "Oh, to think it would have worked" means what I was trying to do, having scammed all these other people in my life, toward the end of my life, I was sort of trying for the ultimate biggie, I was trying to see whether or not I could scam God, and doing it by putting on the robe and the cord of a friar so that if I wore a friar's clothes, then people would think I was a holy man, but more important I could fake out God.

Cook: I'm going to put on my Franciscan suit, and I think I'm going to have it made, but then, as it turns out, Boniface VIII was involved in a very serious military activity in the Papal states against another one of these Roman families, an enemy family of his family, the Colona family. Remember, again, talking about all of these family politics with regard to the papacy, think back to the family politics and the papacy in Inferno 19, Nicholas III and Boniface by anticipation. So he's involved in this war, and the Colona are holed up in the city of Palestrina. If you've ever been there it's way up on top of a mountain; it would be a very hard place to take. So, Boniface wants to capture this city, and just having enough weapons and soldiers won't do it, largely because of where it's located. He needs a sly old fox to tell him how to take Palestrina, and so he calls on Guido da Montefeltro. That's Brother Guido da Montefeltro.

Herzman: Brother Guido, he says that telling us in this narrative, the problem was he was not in the business of doing that kind of stuff anymore. He has a kind of elaborate way of saying it, but he says as follows,

> 'As Constantine (another character who recurs a lot
>   throughout the *Commedia*) once had Silvestro
>   brought
>   from Mount Soracte to cure his leprosy,
>   so this one sought me out as his physician
>
> to cure his burning fever caused by pride.
>   He asked me to advise him. I was silent,
>   for his words were drunken.'

What Boniface wants is advice on how you zap your enemies, and Guido is saying, "Well, I can't give that kind of advice now. I'm not in the advice business. I'm in the friar business."

Cook: However, Boniface is not going to give up.

> 'Fear not, I tell you: the sin you will commit,
>   it is forgiven. Now you will teach me how
>   I can level Palestrina to the ground.
>
> Mine is the power, as you cannot deny,
>   to lock and unlock Heaven. Two keys I have,
>   those keys my predecessor, (now resigned as pope) did
>   not cherish.'

Okay, Boniface says, then, "You give me the info as to how to take this," keep in mind, this is a city full of Christians; Palestrina is in Italy. The Colona and all the residents are Christians. "You tell me how to take that city, and you are already forgiven of the sin of telling me how to blow away fellow Christians."

Herzman: Well that's kind of a neat trick. The problem with it, of course, is that it is something that is not in Boniface's power to do. It's not in God's power to do as far as that goes because it's a contradiction of terms—it's nonsense, it's meaningless. If you are to be forgiven, it is because you are repentant, and if you are repentant it can't include the knowledge that I'm going to do this thing. Okay? So, essentially what happens is, the way Guido tells the story, Boniface makes him an offer that he can't refuse, both in terms of the terms of the offer and in terms of the office of the person who's making it, "Hey, I'm pope, I tell you what to do," and he says, "I bought it." Now, he says,

> And when his weighty arguments had forced me
>   to the point that silence seemed the poorer choice,
>   I said: 'Father, since you grant me absolution
>
> for this sin that I find that I must fall into now:
>   ample promise with this scant fulfillment
>   will bring you triumph on your lofty throne.'

Well, first of all nothing particularly weighty about Boniface's argument at all. The argument is arrant nonsense, but he goes for it, and he therefore tells him, "Here's the strategy that you use, what you do is you make a promise and you don't keep it. You promise that there is going to be a kind of truce, and when they all come out of the fortification, you zap them." Nice guy, Guido.

Cook: Now, one thing you might think about is this guy is a Franciscan. What do Franciscans do? Well, if you go back to the founder, Saint Francis of Assisi, what he did was go around and first of all he said, "Peace" to everybody. The second thing he did was to urge everybody to repent from their sins, to come back to God, and, in fact, when the pope approved the Franciscan Order at the beginning of the 13th century, he specifically approved the friars as preachers of penance. You were to go out and call people to ask God to forgive them their sins, to come back to God. That's the friar business, if you will. Guido is a friar. He has repented and confessed, and he takes on this role of friar. If anybody should know that Boniface's argument is totally bogus, not a weighty argument, it's a friar.

Herzman: Now, what happens, of course, is that they use Francis to kind of continue the fate of Guido after he dies. He does what he's supposed to do.

> Saint Francis came to get me when I died,
>   but one of the black Cherubim cried out:
>   'Don't touch him, don't cheat me of what is mine!

> He must come down to join my other servants
> for the false counsel he gave. From then to now
> I have been ready at his hair, because
>
> one cannot be absolved unless repentant,
> nor can one both repent and will a thing
> at once—the one is canceled out by the other.'

Think of what happens here—it's the devil that points out the logic, and more specifically, the flaw in Boniface's logic, and so you have this wonderful comic scene. One way I like to think of it, you have the three of them sort of lined up there. Who is the best theologian? The pope, Boniface VIII; the friar, Guido; or the devil? And it turns out that the devil wins in a slam dunk. It's kind of interesting to see what that says about the state of penance, let's say, in the Church in Dante's time. It's also interesting to think about it in terms of Guido himself. Here's a guy who spends his entire career scamming others, and in what is an obvious scam directed toward himself, he falls for it—hook, line, and sinker. It's very interesting, in other words, to think about the implications of that: Here's this guy who doesn't see the same thing he's been perpetrating all his life when somebody comes back and plays it against him. Again, I think that goes very deeply to Dante's sense of what sin does, that notion that we said very early on about here are the folks that have lost the "good of intellect." It seems to me that you have to look at Guido as a wonderful example of somebody who has lost the good of intellect.

Cook: Why does Dante spend so much time here? Pretty much two entire cantos, two totally different conversations, why is this such an important place? I think if we look at these two characters, Ulysses and Guido da Montefeltro, one of the things we realize is they're both incredibly bright, they're clever, and they're very good at the use of words. They are really people of enormous ability—the ability of leadership, as it turns out. He was a successful military guy for a lot of years as it turns out, and if we thing about that we also realize what a talented guy Dante is, and Dante knows that. It would be stupid for him to deny it, and therefore what are dangers, what are the temptations, what are the things that can happen to people who have great talents, but don't have what we would call the moral fiber to use them well? Those who simply see those talents as a way to advance their own personal agendas, and in that way, it seems to me, this is a very important place for Dante to stop because certainly he must have been someone who felt some of those temptations that Guido and Ulysses do.

Herzman: When we pick up next time, we will go here, from the realm of simple fraud, to what we call complex fraud—fraud against those who deserve a special trust, who have a special trust for us.

Lecture Eleven
The Ultimate Evil

Scope:

In this lecture, our discussion of the Inferno is brought to a close. We look at the ninth circle of hell, that of complex fraud (fraud against those to whom special trust is owed) by examining the story of Ugolino and Ruggieri, told in Cantos 32 and 33. Dante's way of examining terminal evil is through images of cannibalism, which begin with the image of Ugolino gnawing on the head of his archrival, Ruggieri, and continue in the stark and savage tale told by Ugolino. In this tale, many of the key themes of the Inferno are brought together, including once again, the Guelf-Ghibelline struggle. At the end of the Inferno, we see Satan himself, gnawing on the figures of the three traitors Judas, Cassius, and Brutus. In Satan, we see a monstrous parody of the Christian Trinity and, in the punishment of these traitors, we see a continuation of the idea of cannibalism as the ultimate statement of the nature of evil.

Outline

I. The ninth circle, the last in the Inferno, is also a place of punishment for fraud. It is a place not of fire but of damned souls frozen in ice.

   A. Here are portrayed sinners guilty of fraud, but fraud that is more complex than in the eighth *bolgia*: These sinners have also betrayed a special trust, such as family, or country, or guests, or lord.

   B. The ultimate examples are to be found in the three mouths of Satan, the betrayers Judas, Cassius, and Brutus, in the last canto of the Inferno.

II. At the end of 32, we begin the story of Ugolino and Ruggieri.

   A. Ugolino is gnawing on the head of Ruggieri.

   B. Both are encased in ice up to their necks.

   C. Both are guilty of the sin of betrayal, even though only one of them will speak.

D. The story of Ugolino brings together the political and religious controversies in the city of Pisa in the time of Dante.

    1. Ugolino was the Guelf Podestà, or city manager.

    2. Ruggieri was the Ghibelline archbishop.

    3. Together, they plotted to betray Pisa and seize power.

III. Ugolino narrates a horrible story of betrayal, counter-betrayal, and treachery in Canto 33.

    A. Ugolino tells how he was captured and, together with his young children, imprisoned in a tower by Ruggieri.

    B. He describes their slow death by starvation.

    C. He suggests that to forestall starvation, he ate his children.

        1. This is a controversial line for Dante critics.

        2. Evidence for the "cannibalistic" reading can be found in the biblical, classical, and contemporary sources that Dante draws on.

    D. Cannibalism becomes Dante's way of talking about absolute evil.

        1. It can be seen as an inversion of the Christian Eucharist.

        2. It is a "logical" conclusion to the inversions that have characterized the Inferno.

        3. In Dante's vision of hell, the punishment is to get what you want when nothing stands in the way of your evil desires.

IV. Canto 34 brings the Inferno to a close by continuing the image of cannibalism as the figure for radical evil, the inversion of the good of self-donation (charity) as embodied in the Eucharist.

    A. The three heads of Satan are a parody of the Christian trinity.

    B. Three sinners are found in the three mouths of Satan.

    C. Judas is in the center.

    D. Brutus and Cassius are on the sides.

    E. Dante did not know Plutarch's life of Caesar (on which Shakespeare's play is based).

    F. The two ultimate betrayals are of Christ and of the empire.

V. Dante climbs out of the Inferno by going "through" Satan.

    A. At a certain point, he is no longer going down; he has crossed the center of the earth and is climbing up.

B. His last image of hell is of Satan's legs. Satan is upside down.

C. Dante emerges and is once more able to see the stars.

Readings:

Dante, *Inferno*, Cantos 28–34.

John Freccero, *Dante: The Poetics of Conversion*, Chapters 10–11.

Questions to Consider:

1. Why do we find so much imagery of eating in Cantos 32–34?

2. Why does Dante spend so little time in the presence of Lucifer, and why does he not talk to any of the sinners in the center of hell?

3. Is Dante ready to leave hell and begin his ascent?

Lecture Eleven—Transcript
The Ultimate Evil

Herzman: I guess congratulations are in order, we've made it to the bottom of hell, to the ninth circle, to the last place of punishment in Dante's Inferno. As we mentioned at the end of the last lecture, this is the place where fraud is punished also, but a special kind of fraud, what has been named complex fraud because it involves not simply the sin itself, but the sin as directed against those who have a kind of special claim on us, those to whom we owe a special trust—family, or country, or guests, or lord, and what we see when we get to the very end, the ultimate examples of fraud, they are found in the mouth of Satan himself, with Judas, the betrayer of Christ occupying a prominent central place in the central of the three heads of Satan, and the betrayers Brutus and Cassius are the other two mouths. What we're going to do, I guess, is try to get there, but get there by way of talking about one of the most interesting stories in the entire *Commedia*, another one of pairs that Dante brings together for us. We're going to talk a little bit about the story of two guys named Ugolino and Ruggieri.

Cook: Very often when today we talk about hell lightly, we think of it being a place that's hot with lots of fire, hotter than the hinges of hell, we will say about a summer's day, but, in fact, if you think about it, Dante has used fire rather infrequently in his punishments, and, when we get to the bottom of hell, there's no fire at all. In fact, it is ice. It is the coldest place there is, and we want to think about that. When Dante uses fire, he probably has some special reasons for doing it. After all, we can associate the fire of the love of God, and fire as the tongues of fire at Pentecost, and therefore the gift of the Holy Spirit, but down here it's cold, and the sinners are frozen at different depths, into ice. In fact, some of the last sinners he meets are actually totally frozen inside the ice, and therefore he can't communicate with them. So, as we get down to the bottom of hell, it's not hotter than the hinges of hell, it's colder than we can possibly imagine.

Herzman: The sinners themselves encased in this ice are therefore characterized by a kind of immobility, and for the first time we see Dante sort of actively taking part in the punishment of these sinners by not giving them what they want and by sort of treating them rather badly. Again, this is another one of the signs throughout the Inferno that Dante is beginning to learn something, but what's interesting in this particular case, with Ugolino and Ruggieri, is that once again we have another example of a pair of sinners locked together. Remember we started with Paolo and Francesca, who were in one kind of embrace as they were being whirled around in the tempest of lust. We saw as a pair, Farinata and Cavalcante, they both spoke but not at the same time, and as we said pretty emphatically, not recognizing each other's existence. We saw Ulysses and Diomed, and Ulysses is the only one who does any talking. Well, that pattern is continued here. Again, another interesting kind of embrace, if you want to put it that way, because Ugolino is seen munching on the head of Ruggieri, sort of the last example of sinners reminds us of the first, by a kind of interesting and sort of frightening comparison/contrast thing. But, Ugolino is the only one who does any talking to us. Now, this is a very important thing for us to think about, because Ugolino spends a lot of time telling us what an awful and terrible and really inhuman set of actions was performed against him and his family by Ruggieri, but in the process, what he totally fails to do is to point out this little minor detail that he was doing just as much to Ruggieri, and that he's every bit as much implicated in this horrendous sort of cross-current of betrayal and counter-betrayal that this canto is all about. So, before we look at the text we might want to say just a little bit about who these two guys were.

Cook: We're now turning to the city of Pisa, and we're turning to another round of the Guelf/Ghibelline controversy. In fact, Dante is very careful, from the very bottom of hell. Everyplace we go down here at the bottom, we've got Guelfs and Ghibellines together. Now, remember Dante's a Guelf, and sometimes we read in popular Dante criticism that what Dante really wanted to do in writing Inferno was to stick all the guys he didn't like down there, and this is not it at all, that's really to miss the point. The point would be here especially that Dante has to come to understand—dealing with Farinata and Cavalcante, for example—that factionalism in and of itself is a bad thing, a destroyer of community, a destroyer of basic bonds, and Guelfs and Ghibellines are both part of the problem. It's not one is the problem and the other is a solution. So, here's the basic problem that's going on in Pisa about a decade before the *Commedia* is set. Pisa is a Ghibelline stronghold surrounded by Guelf neighbors, such as Florence, for example. But, because of that, various Guelf neighbors are attacking Pisa and taking castles sort of out in the boonies of Pisan territory. So the Archbishop of Pisa, a guy named

Ruggieri, who is a Ghibelline, says, "I've got a clever idea. Why don't we hire a Guelf as our sort of temporary city manager?"—the Italian word is *Podestà,*—"that way he can negotiate with his Guelf buddies and get us a better deal than we can get for ourselves?" So, they hire Ugolino to be the *Podestà* of Pisa, and as soon as Ugolino arrives we start a mutual betrayal. Ruggieri immediately realizes this was a bad idea. He's no longer in power himself, and therefore works to undercut Ugolino's authority. On the other hand, Ugolino says to his Guelf buddies, "Go ahead and take that castle out there, that's okay. I'm not going to come get you, we're Guelf buddies after all." So, he's betraying his office in Pisa just as Ruggieri is betraying Pisa as well, by trying to undercut Ugolino's authority from the beginning. So we've got this scene of mutual betrayal, and Dante takes this well-known story as a way of addressing this question: If you have hatred, factionalism, selfishness, nothing else matters but me, how far can it go? How bad can it get? Both on earth and as it's reflected in the afterlife.

Herzman: To what Bill's said I would like to sort of piggyback one footnote, and that is in addition to the horrible problem of factionalism and where it ultimately leads, this also deals with the other issue that's been coming up pretty consistently in our discussion, and that is the interference of the wrong relationship between sacred and secular, because, of course, Ugolino is a government official and Ruggieri is a Church cardinal. So the two things that Dante seems to be saying are most responsible for the messed up situation of the world in his own time—the factionalism and that distorted relationship between spiritual and secular—both come together here in the story that's told. Remember, it's told only from the point of view of one person, from Ugolino, and he brings it up as though he is, and again I hate to kind of sound this corny, but it really does work, as though he's a kind of after-dinner speaker because there he is, munching on the head of his arch-enemy Ruggieri, and as it says at the very beginning of Canto 33:

> Lifting his mouth from his horrendous meal,
>> the sinner first wiped off his messy lips
>> in the hair remaining on the chewed-up skull,

> then spoke: 'You want me to renew a grief
>> so desperate that just the thought of it,
>> much less the telling, grips my heart with pain;

> but if my words can be a seed to bear
>   the fruit of infamy for this betrayer,
>   who feeds my hunger, then I shall speak—in tears.'

Remember back to the beginning with Francesca, Francesca says, "Speaking, telling my story, it hurts, but I'll do it anyhow because you've asked," and in that we saw the essence of Francesca's sin, she's just a girl who can't say no, right? Here he's saying it hurts, again that deliberate sort of recognition of what happened at the beginning, that imitation of it, it hurts, but I'm going to talk anyhow. Why? I don't care what happens to me as long as I can get him. I will endure anything in order to get my enemy. In a nutshell, that's the essence of sin for Dante. That recognition, that sin ultimately hurts you first, foremost, and above all, but that isn't going stop you. So you see in his desire to tell the story, the nature of the sin is reenacted.

Cook: Another way to say this is to look at what is actually happening down here in hell, frozen in the ice up to their necks, Ugolino munching on the head of Ruggieri. Ron sometimes asks this to our students, "Which one would you rather be?" That is to say, which one really is in the worse situation? To be eaten by another person, or to be eating another human being. It is easy for us, again, because we only have Ugolino's point of view here, to see that Ugolino was in the better situation, but we really ought to ask that question seriously, and I think what we're struck with is the utter horror of both of their positions. Not that Ugolino's a little bit better off, in fact, they are in exactly the same situation even though one is, to use Ron's words, "One is the muncher and one is the munchee."

Herzman: Well, he tells his story, again, leaving out all the parts that implicate himself in the treachery, and tells it in such a way that it is meant to evoke the greatest possible amount of sort of pity and terror on the part of the listener, and one of the reasons why it probably should provide us with that kind of reaction is because it wasn't just about Ugolino and Ruggieri going after each other, it's about the innocent people who got in the way and suffered because of it, and in this case it turns out to be Ugolino's children. Once Ugolino is arrested, so to speak, and put in this tower, his children are put in there with him, and so what Ugolino decides to do is to sort of focus his story on the suffering of his children. Now as a kind of strategy to get our pity, it works. As a strategy to sort of see what a bad guy Ruggieri is, it works, but, of course, it also works to put the blame on Ugolino himself, who is equally responsible for the whole situation, and it also works to make a point that Dante is clearly interested in making, namely the problem with all this evil stuff is that lots of innocent people get dragged down with it, and the image for that, in going back to biblical times, of course, is what happens to innocent children? The suffering of innocent children as a kind of image of the consequences of radical evil continues from then to Dante, and all the way beyond until now.

Cook: When we met up with Francesca and Paolo in Inferno 5, one of the things we said is we really have to dissect her story very carefully because if we don't, if we simply take her at her word, we're going to misunderstand radically what's going on. Maybe that seemed like a kind of leisurely activity when we're dealing with Francesca. It's absolutely dead serious down here. That is to say, if we take Ugolino at his own terms as he expects us to understand him, we're going to miss an extraordinarily powerful lesson about the nature of sin, about the nature of evil, that hopefully we have developed the skills as readers, starting with that Francesca encounter, so that we can see that these speakers are telling us more than they think they are about themselves if we are discerning readers. Dante had problems in the beginning, if you recall, in misinterpreting Francesca, and we no doubt felt sympathy for that. Now we are down here in the bottom of hell, and Dante understands what's going on, and so must we. So we hope we've honed our skills as we've journeyed with the pilgrim and hear this story, because as the story begins to unfold, they're not only in prison, but one day Ugolino realized they are nailing the door closed. They are nailing the door—through which they were fed—closed, and Ugolino almost immediately understands what that means, and therefore the dramatic story that he unfolds is what happens after the nailing up of the door of the tower in Pisa.

Herzman: Of course, what happens is he realizes to a degree that his children don't, that they are being slowly starved to death, again, a kind of consequence of a radical betrayal, and he tells it in terms of slow but inevitable movement toward starvation. The helplessness that he feels as a parent when all of a sudden they're hungry, asking for food, there's nothing that he can do. Also, just sort of death-by-death he recounts what happens to his children.

'...It was around the time
    they usually brought our food to us. But now
    each one of us was full of dread from dreaming;

then from below I heard them driving nails
    into the dreadful tower's door; with that,
    I stared in silence at my flesh and blood.

I did not weep, I turned to stone inside;
    they wept, and my little Anselmuccio spoke:
    'What is it, father? Why do you look that way?'

For them I held my tears back, saying nothing,
    all of that day, and then all of that night,
    until another sun shone on the world.

A meager ray of sunlight found its way
    to the misery of our cell, and I could see
    myself reflected four times in their faces;'

Well, he continues, they offer, the children do, to feed their father with their own flesh. He refuses that. They die one by one, and then he picks it up with the account of his own death.

'...Just as you see me here,
    I saw the other three fall one by one,
    as the fifth day and the sixth day passed. And I,

by then gone blind, groped over their dead bodies.
    Though they were dead, two days I called their name.
    Then hunger proved more powerful than grief.'

Well, what is it that Ugolino is saying here?

Cook: Although scholars have disputed that question for centuries, it seems to us that what Ugolino says is, "I ate them." That he simply had hunger being more powerful than grief, and therefore to sustain his life just a little bit longer, after all he ate his own children. There's this image of cannibalism back on earth in Pisa, and of course it's reflected in the cannibalism down in hell of Ugolino munching on the head of Ruggieri. One of the things that always strikes me is, as Ugolino moves in to sort of the final phase of telling this story, he says to Dante, "Aren't you weeping? If you don't weep at my story, do you ever weep?" And yet, just a few lines later, he says, "And when I was confronted with this and my children, I did not weep." Ron read the line. "I had turned to stone inside." What an odd notion that this is the story that should invoke weeping from anyone. It didn't invoke weeping from him. Now, one could sort of read this as sort of the stoic father, but I don't think that's it. He's turned to stone inside, that the kind of life he's led, the kind of betrayal that he's carried out, the kind of real sort of leave every human consideration out in the wheeling and dealing of castles and politics and all this sort of stuff, he's become stone, and at a time when his children need him, and this emotional bond should be as tight as it possibly could be, he tells us he's made of stone.

Herzman: It's interesting in particular because that idea of having a heart of stone is something that is presented very specifically in the prophet Ezekiel. If we look at the other prophets, remember we told you in earlier lectures how important they are to Dante's sensibility, one of the things that's very interesting is to see how often they refer to images of cannibalism when it becomes time to talk about what happens when there's nothing left whatsoever of the Covenant, that the absolute betrayal of the Covenant leads to—or is imaged by—cannibalism. So there's a kind of connection between what's happening here on earth, what's happening here in hell, and what's happening here with the prophets, all sort of brought together in a very powerful way. And, again, if you begin thinking about this, in addition to the biblical authors, we can also bring in classical authors as well. One of the things that is kind of interesting when you think about cannibalism as an image is the way in which it is the father eating children in particular; it is sort of the absolute denial of the idea of *pietas*, the idea of loyalty that we've already talked about as being so important in defining who Aeneas is. That Aeneas is who he is because of the set of relationships he has to father and son. Ulysses is who he is by the denial of that set of relationships. Here you have the kind of ultimate denial of that set of relationships with a father munching on his children, and then going back to picking it up by munching on his enemy here in hell. In other words, what is so nifty about the dramatic power of this line is that when he tells that final line in his story, the story is over but he immediately goes back to the meal that he's having, the eternal meal, munching on the head of his arch-enemy, the archbishop. Well, that becomes a kind of nifty way to suggest that maybe, to follow up with what Bill said a few minutes ago, maybe being the "munchee" is no worse than being the "muncher." That is to say, by going back to that meal on Ruggieri's head, he is eternally reenacting his final act on earth, the one that is the total denial and betrayal of any kind of love whatsoever, and so in a way, it's kind of as though two things are happening at the same time. Doing this he's punishing himself in this extraordinary way, and he's also getting exactly what he wanted. One of the things that this canto seems to me to be all about is that if you think about what you would love to do to your worst enemy, beyond anything else you could ever think of, "Gosh, I'd like to be able to munch on his head," he gets to—he gets to do exactly what he wants, and in Dante's vision of hell, the punishment is really to get what you want when nothing stands in the way of your desires, and if nothing stands in the way of your desires, what you have is a kind of cannibalism as an image for ultimate and final evil.

Cook: One way to contextualize this politically, something Ron alluded to earlier, is to say, "If you took sort of the partisan politics of Farinata and Cavalcante, and again said, 'How far can that go?'" Remember, they simply sort of ignore each other even though they are neighbors for eternity in the same tomb. How far could you go? How far could you push that? Where will ultimately the attitudes that we see in other sinners and in the world of partisan politics, where will it lead? How far can it go when all of a sudden, me, power, control, are all that matter, and the most fundamental bonds are broken, bonds with my neighbor, bonds with my government, bonds with my family, bonds with God. Everything is sacrificed here to this desire that as Ron said, is totally out of control. It's also a matter of saying something like this: "What, if you look at a world, and you see nothing simply but politics and physical objects and whatever." That's a totality reality. There's no spirit. Not just in a technical theological sort of term, but there's nothing except stuff, and collecting power, and collecting things. Well, it's interesting because it's an image that develops in Chapter Six in John's Gospel, where Jesus is saying, "I am the bread of life, and you must eat my body and drink my blood." Obviously not talking literally, but in spirit. But some of the people around respond, "Ooh, this is more than we can stomach." In other words, if you listen to those words literally, they're cannibalism. If you fill those words full of spirit, they're this intimate union with your Lord. What happens when that whole spiritual dimension is eradicated?

Herzman: Of course, what that means is that Dante is bringing in the resonances that would have been available to him as a Christian, that in Dante's Christian world, the way that you show love is through a banquet, the Eucharist, in which you are eating the body and blood of Christ. Well, it shows, of course, as Bill said, the necessity of spiritual understanding in that meal, but it also shows the kind of nifty inversion that's going on here. As Bill put it, what you have is the letter without the spirit of that banquet, and the letter without the spirit turns out to be cannibalism.

Cook: It's also interesting that the final sinners Dante meets before he gets to Satan himself later on in Inferno 33 describe back on earth a banquet. They invited their family for dinner. They had a code word, and when it was time for dessert, the servants came in and slaughtered the members of the family. So we go from this banquet of Ugolino and Ruggieri to another one, and then when Dante finally does come face-to-face with Satan, there's still another banquet because, as Ron pointed out in the beginning of the lecture, Satan has three heads and in each one is a sinner being chewed.

Herzman: Of course, that's the vision that Dante sees in Canto 34, the last canto of the Inferno. He gets to have a meeting, if that's the right word, a face-to-face with Satan. Now, again, it's kind of interesting to see in terms of what has already come along, the way that this meeting is sort of put together. It makes sense that there wouldn't be any direct encounter, any dialogue between Dante and Satan, and, in fact, there's nothing intelligible coming from Satan at all. Dante looks and is sort of stupefied by what he sees, and it seems to be the sort of unstated and sort of very real sense that we'd better get out of here pretty quickly before we sort of take part in this nuclear meltdown works of evil, but what you do get to see is a kind of interesting way of summing up what the entire infernal experience has been. In a sense, what we can do is look at the image of Satan as a kind of image that puts the seal on everything that we've seen, starting when we went through the gates of hell and going all the way down to the very end.

Cook: One way to do it is to remember that in the mythology that Dante's using, Satan led a rebellion in which he got some other angels to participate against God himself in heaven, and God sort of flung him down, and he's stuck in the middle of the earth. Well, remember some of the first folks, some of the first things, we met in

Inferno 3, when we went through the gates of hell, were those angels who remained neutral during the rebellion, that wouldn't take any side at all. Here's the leader of the rebellion much further down, so that's one connection between the beginning of our entrance into hell, and the end here in Inferno 34.

Herzman: There is a whole bunch of other ways to take a look at Satan. One of them is that because there is no intellectual content, that you can see that ultimately all of the masks of evil are very frightening, but evil itself in the final analysis is impotent against Dante. Nonetheless, he observes who the greatest traitors are, and then moves on, and I suppose it is up to us all to say something about the three final traitors, because, of course, they are the three—the winners of the kind of "who are the greatest sinners of all time" contest in 1300. It turned out to be Judas, and it turned out to be Brutus and Cassius. It's probably easiest to see what Judas is all about there, he betrays Christ and, again, with a kind of interesting cannibalistic image here, he is being eaten by Satan's central mouth. We see his feet sticking out, but the other two sinners in the other mouths, Brutus and Cassius, might not be quite so obvious to a contemporary reader, especially if it is a reader who comes to these folks through, let's say, reading Shakespeare's version of this story in *Julius Caesar*.

Cook: Well, for Dante, the Roman Republic was leading to empire, because Dante believed in the ideal of empire, in the ideal of world government where there wouldn't be any competition for power, therefore power would be used wisely because there was nothing to be gained by using it poorly, or badly. So, for Dante, Julius Caesar was the one to bring the empire into being in Rome. However, of course, Brutus and Cassius thwarted that effort, and it took another round of civil wars and another generation before Augustus emerged as the emperor, and Dante believed that God would not send the world a savior until the world was at peace with one government. So, the murder of Julius Caesar not only cost a lot of lives and another round of civil wars, but it also postponed God's plan. It messed up the plan as it was going. So, they were also working against heaven's design, just as Judas was. It's hard, I guess Ron said, to know that this was the "noblest Roman of them all" stuff, to understand that Dante's operating in a very different worldview than Plutarch, the source for Shakespeare's *Julius Caesar*.

Herzman: The last thing we have to do in Inferno is get out of it, and it's not as easy as it sounds, because, of course, you are at the very bottom, but remember that Satan himself is encased in ice. Fortunately, there is a little hole there, and Dante and Virgil kind of slip by the hole and are going along the legs of Satan, and all of a sudden realize that instead of going down they're going up. So, his last view really is to see the legs of Satan. There is sort of a pathway all the way up, and it ends with Dante and Virgil, as it said,

> We climbed, he first and then I behind, until,
> through a small round opening ahead of us
> I saw the lovely things the heavens hold,
>
> and we came out to see once more the stars.

Well, in the next lectures, we will take a look at things where the stars are visible and where light is visible, and we'll move to purgatory.

Lecture Twelve
The Seven-Story Mountain

Scope:

In this lecture, we begin by discussing the idea of purgatory as it developed over the course of the Christian tradition before Dante's time. Dante himself is the most important figure in the development of our modern imagery for purgatory, as well as the idea of purgatory as a place of spiritual growth that readies the soul for the vision of God in heaven. We discuss the structure of purgatory, a mountain with seven terraced stories in which all of the seven tendencies toward sin—called the seven deadly sins—are successively purged. The reader gets a sense of the kind of place purgatory is, and how it is different from hell, by looking at the guardian of purgatory, Cato of Utica, in Canto 1; Casella, an old friend of Dante's in Canto 2; and Manfred, bastard son of the Emperor Frederick II, in Canto 3.

Outline

I. We begin the second canticle of the *Commedia*, Purgatory, by a discussion of the idea and the history of purgatory.

    A. Dante himself, through this very poem, is the figure most responsible for the image we have of purgatory.

    B. The idea of purgatory, however, goes back much further to the Church fathers.

    C. There is not a great deal of direct scriptural warrant for purgatory.

II. Purgatory is a place of communal repentance, reflecting the reality of sin as damage not only to the sinner but to others as well. Cooperation and mutual support exist in purgatory as the souls work together for moral improvement.

    A. The idea was developed in the early Church to deal with what happens to sinners who repent but have not fully turned to God before they died.

    B. Purgatory, unlike heaven or hell, is a place of change. In this way, it resembles earth.

    C. It is, therefore, the place where sinners are purified so that they become ready to see God.

D. The punishments of purgatory have purgation as their purpose.

E. Although purgatory may in some of its outward manifestations resemble hell, for Dante it is closer to being an anteroom of heaven than an annex of hell. Everyone in purgatory is heaven-bound but must be perfected first.

F. The gatekeeper of purgatory is Cato of Utica (also called Cato the Stoic, d. 46 B.C.E.), a pagan, a suicide, and an enemy of Caesar (he killed himself rather than become Caesar's captive and, thus, became an emblem of republican liberty).

G. That Dante places Cato among the saved shows that the *Commedia* is not a puzzle to be solved but a mystery to be experienced.

III. According to Dante, the geography of purgatory consists of a mountain that was created when God cast Lucifer into the center of the earth, thus forcing to the earth the matter displaced by the fall.

A. Dante constructs purgatory on this mountain.

B. It consists of three parts: antepurgatory, where the late repentant wait because they made God wait; purgatory proper, seven terraces on the mountain; and the earthly paradise, which is at the top of the mountain.

C. The seven terraces of purgatory proper are arranged as places of communal purgation for each of the seven deadly sins.

    1. Dorothy L. Sayers said, "to know Dante and the *Commedia* only through Inferno is like knowing the city of Paris only through its sewer system."

    2. Purgatory reveals the truth of this observation even in its earliest cantos.

D. The seven deadly sins are those tendencies at the root of our being that keep us from focusing on God and the good.

E. The ordering that Dante uses is pride, envy, anger, sloth, avarice, gluttony, and lust.

IV. We learn about the kind of place purgatory is from some of the inhabitants that we meet early on.

A. Cato of Utica is the first.

B. Casella, an old musician friend of Dante's, sings one of the "oldies but goodies" for Dante, putting to music one of Dante's own poems in Canto 2.

   1. Cato rebukes him and says that the pilgrim must move on.

   2. We learn the importance of going forward rather than backward.

C. In Canto 3, Dante meets Manfred (d. 1266), a bastard son of the Emperor Frederick II and a violent arch-Ghibelline.

   1. Manfred was killed at the Battle of Bevenento, a Guelf victory.

   2. Manfred was an enemy of Dante's family and party. The Guelf victory at Bevenento led directly to the Alighieri family's return to Florence.

   3. It is a real surprise to see him among the saved.

   4. We learn of the power of a final conversion at the end of life.

   5. We also learn that salvation does not depend on family affiliation.

Readings:

William Cook and Ronald Herzman, *The Medieval World View*, Chapters 7–9.

Dante, *Purgatorio*, Cantos 1–3.

Rachel Jacoff, ed., *The Cambridge Companion to Dante*, Chapter 12.

Questions to Consider:

1. Why does this non-eternal part of the afterlife receive as much attention from Dante as heaven and hell?

2. How is purgatory different from both heaven and hell?

3. How does the presence of Cato and Manfred tell the readers that we have a lot left to learn?

Lecture Twelve—Transcript
The Seven-Story Mountain

Cook: There is a lot of talk about heaven and hell in the Bible. They are the places of eternity in the afterlife. But, in fact, the word "purgatory" never appears. Therefore, we have to ask, not just what is purgatory like, but why is it here at all? Why does it get equal time with hell and paradise in Dante's scheme of the afterlife? Instead of sort of starting with a theological argument, let me start with a sort of practical problem that exists. Let's assume that hell is a place for unrepentant sinners, and heaven is a place for those who are not only repentant, but cleaned entirely from sin. Only pure people go to heaven. Now here's my situation. I steal 100 dollars from Ron Herzman. He doesn't know it. One night I just can't get to sleep I'm so upset; I've come to the realization that I've done something wrong; it's a terrible thing. I've sinned against God and neighbor, and I want to do something about it. So, I start the process by saying "I'm really sorry," and tomorrow I'm going to do a couple of things—I'm going to give him the 100 dollars back, and I'm going to go to church and talk to my priest, and the next morning, I walk out of my house and get run over by a truck. What happens? Well, I can't go to hell really because I am sorry, but I can't go to heaven because I'm not purified. I may have started the process of purification, but I haven't completed it, and this sort of silly story is at least one way of answering the question, "Why purgatory?"

Herzman: I think we can continue with it. What Bill said, of course, deals with one aspect of this idea of repentance. The problem is that Bill went to his reward, and he still owed me 100 bucks. What happens, in other words, is a sort of idea of justice about all of this stuff that is left undone when you die sorry for your sins, but unable, really, to make a kind of reparation or restitution for them. Of course, there's also the complicated problem of a lot of sins being of the sort that you can't make restitution for them at all because of the nature of the sin itself. It's certainly possible, had he lived, to pay me back the 100 bucks, maybe even a little interest, but supposing he got into a fit of rage at some terrible Dante comment that I made, and he decided to kill me. Well, it's harder to restitution for that one. So, again, purgatory can be looked at, at least in part, as a place that deals with the restitution that you were not able to accomplish back on earth. But also, in addition to this sort of public dimension of sin, that is to say, the fact that our sins really do affect other people, they are also sins directly against God, and they are also actions, which, as we saw in the Inferno, turn out to mostly impact the people who commit them. In other words, if you are going to the afterlife with all of the effects of sin in your own being, you're not really ready for the vision of God; you're not really ready for the bliss of paradise, and so, one way to take a look at purgatory is as the place that gets you ready for bliss. Purgatory is the place where you learn how to see God face-to-face, by learning that's really ultimately what you ought to be looking for, and not other things that in your life have given you various sorts of satisfactions. The folks in hell have learned that the only source of their bliss is going to be themselves, and that is what they get for eternity. Well, we have this kind of instinct toward the selfish, if you will. Augustine would probably put it some way like that, this instinct to create idols for ourselves. Purgatory is the place where we are purged of all of those tendencies.

Cook: One thing we need to understand about purgatory that sometimes is misunderstood is, every soul in purgatory ends up in heaven. Purgatory is temporal, hell and heaven are both eternal. So, when you sail up to the shore of the mountain of purgatory, you are going to be saved. It may happen by simply climbing what Dante will describe as this mountain step-by-step until the purgation process is completed, or if you are there at the time of the Last Judgment, all the souls in purgatory will go immediately to heaven, and purgatory in eternity will be empty. It's a place you pass through; it's nobody's eternal destination, and that's going to make it a very different place than either hell or heaven.

Herzman: Notice that it also means, to key back on what Bill has just said, that ultimately it is impossible to flunk purgatory. That is to say, souls there are not being tested to see whether they're going to go back down or continue up—they're all going to make it. One reason that it's sort of necessary to emphasize that is the fact that purgatory itself consists of a number of punishments. Purgatory is not a walk in the park in a lot of its specific mechanisms. We see people there who are intensely suffering as a way of repentance. If you look at it, therefore, only in terms of surface of the two places, it seems to have a lot in common with hell. The fact is, that the deeper you go, the fewer the similarities, and it makes a whole lot more sense to think about purgatory as the anteroom, the vestibule of heaven, than it does to think about it as a sort of annex for hell. That it really is part of heaven in a way that is made, in fact, very emphatic because you go through a gate to get there; that's the last gate you really go through until you get to heaven itself. So, it's important to keep these initial distinctions in mind because they have everything to do with the kinds of activities that go on in purgatory.

Cook: The temporal nature of purgatory has a lot of implications for us. First of all, it means it's a place where there is change. There's really no change in hell. Those souls are doing the same thing forever. There's no change in heaven; they are present with the vision of God forever. But, purgatory is a place of change. It's measured by night and day, if you will; hell is only night, and heaven is only day. It's also a place where the pilgrims themselves change and grow as they advance up the mountain of purgatory, and Dante, therefore, goes through essentially the same process in purgatory as the souls do that are there. So, it's sort of more like earth in some ways than either heaven or hell. We have a story to tell you about our inmates whom we taught years ago at Attica Prison. We asked them what's their favorite part of the *Divine Comedy* when they finished the course, and for most students it seems the answer is "Inferno," enough beasties and strange encounters, and whatever. And, perhaps the monks, when we taught them at a Trappist Abbey their answer was "paradise," but the answer for the inmates was "purgatory" because they recognized a central element of purgatory. It's a place of moral improvement, and these guys in their condition said they could identify more with the souls and with Dante the pilgrim in purgatory than either the souls and Dante in hell or the souls and Dante in paradise.

Herzman: Notice that if Dante is improving, and the souls are improving also, this is sort of a radical difference from what the pilgrim Dante has to undergo in hell, because there his job was to learn how to be unlike as possible the folks that were there. What he had to learn to see in them was a series of negative examples, "ghosts of Christmas future;" don't do that or that's where you're going to wind up. Here, he's doing it together with them as Bill suggests, and this, too, is suggestive of another very important aspect of purgatory, namely that repentance itself turns out to be a communal rather than an individual activity, that as we said so many times in hell, people are reenacting the fact that they have made themselves the center of the universe, and there is no room for anybody else. Isolation is the name of the game throughout. But here, what happens is that much that gets done can only get done when people are acting together, acting in concert, and learning how to do that is one of the main tasks of the souls who are there.

Cook: Before we actually journey up the mountain, we need to also lay down this principle. It's very easy, and many college students do this, to read Inferno and say, "Well, I understand what Dante is saying, I get his view of this and that and the other thing, with regard to love, or sodomy, or bad popes, or whatever might be, got it." However, as soon as we get to the shore of purgatory in Purgatorio 1, we recognize right away that, in fact, we don't have all of Dante's answers. We've got what Ron often calls "Dante's first offer" in Inferno. Think that pagans can't go anywhere but limbo? That's the best place that they can go? Well, we're going to find out differently. Think people that are being kicked out of the Church are not going to be saved? We've got to think that one out again very quickly. So we need to remember that we do not know the whole scheme yet. We've got part of what Dante wants to tell us, and one of the first things is sort of the "we're not in Kansas anymore" kind of response because not only is the terrain different, not only do the souls act differently, but the people we encounter here, especially toward the bottom of purgatory, are folks that you just, you know, if I gave you their life history you'd just bet your bottom buck they'd be somewhere in hell.

Herzman: Okay, we want to, in fact, emphasize the way in which Dante presents us with figures who are deliberately meant to kind of tease us into the "you're not in Kansas anymore" attitude. That is to say, all of these folks that we see at the beginning seem to have in common a sense that, "wait a minute, wait a minute, you are a bad guy!"—so remember that in this notion of communal repentance, the first thing that you need to keep in mind is that any sin, properly confessed and recanted, will allow for repentance. There is no such thing as the sin that is too bad or too awful to be forgiven, and what Dante does, I think, at the beginning, is in challenging the expectations that built up in Inferno, suggest to us that this must mean that the folks who are in Inferno are those who have refused to take advantage of an opportunity to repent. I think that is very important. We've talked about Inferno is a place where people are there because they want to be there. Inferno is really a place where if God came down and said, "I'm going to let you out," you would drag yourself kicking and screaming so that he couldn't do that to you. But it's also interesting to see that when we get to purgatory, that these are people who have been given the option. Bill said that for our prisoners it was a place of hope, really, for them. One of the things that signifies this hope is the notion that they can be saved no matter how bad their sins are against all expectations, at the last minute, even though they've been excommunicated. There's a whole list of things that would seem to be tugging in the other direction, and the beginning of Purgatorio is ultimately, they don't count. They are not as strong as God's mercy; they are not as strong as the desire that God has that people be saved. That's one of the lessons that we see in the early cantos, sort of preparatory to the actual climb up the mountain itself.

Cook: Ready for a test? Let's try this one: Where do you think in the afterlife a person belongs who is a) a pagan who lived and died before the time of Christ, b) a person who committed suicide, c) an enemy of Julius Caesar who was to be the first emperor in Rome? Well, again, all of what we know so far suggests the answer is hell, and, in fact, we could pick out a variety of places to put that person, and yet that is, in fact, the first person whom Dante and Virgil encounter on the shore of purgatory, a person called Cato, sometimes called Cato the Stoic, who died in 46 B.C. by his own hand, at the end of the civil war between Pompey and Julius Caesar.

Herzman: Cato seems to be a guy who had that Roman sternness as part of his character, and so as a kind of keeper of the grounds, a sort of the doorman to purgatory, he seems like he's an apt figure. Again, as Bill points out, all of the things that Cato did in his life would seem to be exactly the sort of thing that, gosh, at best, let's put this guy back there with the virtuous pagans. So the very first person that he meets is there saying, "Guess what fans? The 'rules' are very different here," and Cato sort of responds to the souls who show up. There is a wonderful set of lines at the beginning when we're talking about what happens in purgatory. "May it please you to welcome him—he goes / in search of freedom…" This is Virgil speaking to Cato about why he should sort of welcome Dante onto the shores of the Mount of Purgatory, a little desert island, with the Mountain of Purgatory rising up out of it. There's Cato, and Virgil says, "Let this guy in," and despite all of Cato's firmness, ultimately he's there to let people in rather than to keep people out. He's also there to see that once you're there, there's no fooling around. He's a kind of the guardian of purgatory as a marine Drill Instructor. He's there to kind of kick some butt as well. Dante chose well in choosing somebody who could keep things moving here, but the important thing to see about him is he, too, is going to be saved, and this amazing paradox that Cato, somebody who did not really influence Dante, not somebody he owed a big amount to for his own study of the Roman world, is saved. Virgil, his guide, his master, ultimately is going to go back down into the limbo of the virtuous pagans. So, surprise number one, Cato as guardian.

Cook: We need to be aware of the fact that it's sometimes easy to read, I suppose, any major work of literature, especially something with all the historical references of Dante, as a puzzle to be studied. If I can just either read enough footnotes or make up enough of my own, I'll understand this poem, and if we start with that, rather than seeing in some real way that this poem is a mystery to be experienced, we will be lesser readers, and find lesser joy and meaning in the poem. There is mystery, and Dante increasingly— through purgatory, and more so in heaven—will remind us of the fact that however much he learns all the way though his journey, it does not eliminate mystery; it does not eliminate the need for trust.

Herzman: One aspect of Cato, I think, is worth concerning. Bill mentioned all the aspects of his life that would tend to move you to seeing him in hell rather than purgatory. The fact is that, as Bill said, he committed suicide rather than accept the rule of Julius Caesar. It seems that this is a case where Dante the poet is willing to accept Cato's suicide on its own terms. In other words, it is not a flight away from life itself. I'm not going to live life if I can't do it on my own terms the way in which it happened, let's say, with Pier delle Vigne, in Inferno 13, but rather a statement of a kind of principle, "All right, I'm not going to give into this," which seems almost as though it links itself in some way with actions of Christian martyrs, so that Dante is willing to accept Cato's suicide on its own terms, as something which, by his lights, turned out to be a virtuous act, and therefore, also to show us exactly how important motive is in the final disposition of all of the people that we see in the afterlife.

Cook: In Canto 2, Dante and Virgil are joined by some people, some souls, who have newly arrived at the base of the Mountain of Purgatory. Since Dante knows one of these folks, he says, "You died several months ago, what took you so long to get here?" The answer was that I should have been delaying things, so God delayed things a bit, a principle that operates through a good deal of the beginning of purgatory. Then he says, "Now the boats are ferrying souls all the time because of a jubilee year that's been proclaimed in Rome, and that's allowing folks to just come here right away, and not have to wait. It's a wonderful thing." What's interesting to us here, the jubilee year—the first, by the way, in Christian history—was proclaimed by Pope Boniface VIII. He is the reason, if you will, that some of these souls are arriving here more quickly than they would otherwise. Now, I don't think Dante's backing off his condemnation of Boniface, but it does suggest first of all that Boniface is a pope who has certain power, and even though Boniface might have called the jubilee year to get more tourist dollars in Rome or whatever it is, the bottom line is, it has good consequences, and so even here, with this nemesis Boniface VIII, we still, to some extent, say we're going at least to be seeing things from a broader perspective, and a somewhat different angle than we did in Inferno.

Herzman: Once again, that sense that what you see in Inferno is only Dante's first offer. You should never take that as final. It just occurs to me, this might be a good time to say one of my favorite quotes about Inferno. Dorothy L. Sayers, whose translation we mentioned and whose criticism is actually well worth reading, said "to understand Dante and his *Commedia* only through Inferno is like knowing the city of Paris only through its sewer system." It seems to me that we get all kinds of clues to that right here in the beginning, but we should be aware of others. There is constant expansion and revision of things that have gone on before. Anyhow, this guy, Casella, that we meet, who has been sort of speeded up in his process by the jubilee, turns out to be somebody Dante knew, was a buddy of Dante's back in the old days, and was something of a fairly famous musician. Just to sort of say in passing that we're going to meet a lot of people who are connected with poetry, music, and the arts—in both general and specific ways—from the beginning of purgatory all the way to the end, and we'll make note of that as we go on, but this first poet that he says, this first musician, again those two categories would not be as separate as they are in our own time, turns out to be somebody who has apparently known Dante, but put one of Dante's own poems to music.

Cook: So Dante says to Casella, "Hey, let's have a little tune. Let's sit down, and let's just have an old jam session like we had back in the old days," and so Casella agrees and decides to sing a song. It's interesting because the song turns out to be a song whose words are Dante's.

Herzman: So, this is kind of an interesting thing, in the poem written by Dante, a character in the poem named Casella says, "Here's my favorite golden oldie, okay, this one was top of the charts for a long time," and he begins in the music translation, and it's kept in the Italian, "*amor che ne la mente mi ragiona*, / began the words of his sweet melody." So, we're hearing one of Dante's own poems set to music by Casella, and as soon as this happens, Cato comes running up to the two of them and says, "What the heck are you guys doing? Cut that stuff out and get ready for your journey." It's sort of interesting to ask why he's so stern there. Is he saying, "Dante, all that poetry stuff that you did in the past doesn't mean anything?" or is he saying, "Maybe the stuff that you did in the past is not totally appropriate for what's going on now; we have to kind of push ourselves ahead." Well, it seems that there's a really interesting clue to this that takes place a little bit earlier in the canto when we hear a group of souls who are also singing as they arrive on the Mountain of Purgatory.

Cook: They're singing together; it's not a performance, and what they are singing is Psalm 114, which begins and is quoted here in Latin, "*In exitu Israël de Aegypto*," when Israel came out of Egypt. That is to say it's a Psalm that retells the story of the Exodus, and if you recall at the beginning of our course, we said that the Exodus is just sort of a paradigmatic event. It's the journey from slavery to freedom. It's a journey from exile to the homeland. It's a journey from death to life. It's no accident that they are singing this Psalm together as they begin their process of purgation, because, as we know, the Exodus does serve as this great model, not just for the Christian life, but for Dante's specific journey as Ron outlined it in an earlier lecture.

Herzman: So, what we have in Canto 2 are essentially two songs that frame the canto. The first, the Psalm, the song of communal repentance, the song that really recreates the journey that Dante himself is on. Later on, we have a song of Dante's own poetic career, and we're basically told, "Hey, put that on hold while you move ahead." So, it becomes a kind of framing device to tell us that what purgatory is all about is leaving some things behind, taking some things with you for the journey, and most important trying to figure out which belongs to which category, and so in two cantos, we have some of the rules of the game under our belt.

Cook: You might be asking, "Well, when do we actually get to the so-called Seven-Story Mountain, the way that Dante describes the purgation process? Surprisingly, the answer is not till we're more than a quarter of the way through purgatory. Up to that time, we have various sections of what's sometimes called antepurgatory, a place where those who kept God waiting are themselves waiting for the purgation process to begin. So, we don't just leap onto these seven terraces of the mountain, but rather we have a number of very important encounters before we actually get to the gate through which they must pass in order to get to the actual seven terraces. In Canto 3, Dante meets up with another figure we probably wouldn't expect to find here. He meets up with a guy named Manfred. Manfred turns out to be the son of the Emperor Frederick II. He's the one who carried on Frederick II's military and political ambitions, therefore sort of the great boo-hoo of the Ghibelline world after Frederick dies in 1250. He's a Ghibelline, he's a pretty violent guy, and in those struggles with the papacy, he was excommunicated. He was killed in 1266, at the Battle of Bevenento, a battle, in fact, that led direction to the Guelf return in Florence. Something that was good for Dante, given the fact that he was one-year-old and his family was Guelf. Nevertheless, we meet up with Manfred, who tells us an extraordinary story about the last minutes of his life.

Herzman: The first thing that he does is ask Dante if he recognizes him. Now, Manfred was a pretty famous guy, but Dante doesn't, and it is sort of interesting; it doesn't throw him into a fit, as it would have, let's say, for a character like Farinata in hell, or, in fact, any of them who were sort of obsessed with their own name and their own fame. Here's this guy who was very famous then; there's a kind of obscurity now, and, again, to pick it up in the text,

> When I, (Dante the pilgrim is speaking) in all humility confessed,
> I did not recognize him, he said: 'Look,'
> as he revealed a gash above his breast.

> Then with a smile he said, 'Manfred I am,
> grandson of Emperor Constance, and I beg you,
> when you are with the living once again,

> go to my lovely child, mother of kings
> > who honor Sicily and Aragon;
> > whatever may be rumored, tell her this:'

Then he tells the story of his own death.

Now, the first thing that I think is kind of interesting is the question of "Why is this man smiling?" What is there about his situation that would warrant a smile? Our take on this is that it's an awareness on Manfred's part, this sort of I'm the last guy that you expected to see here among the saved. I bet you thought that I'd be back down there, and sort of happy about this situation, but also not boasting about who he is in any way, perfectly happy to just say, "Here I am, I'm Manfred, let me tell you my story," not because the story paints him in a particularly attractive light, but rather because of what the story does is say something about the mercy of God. It's what the rest of it is really all about.

Cook:

> 'As I lay there, (dying on the battlefield of Bevenento) my
> > body torn by these
> > two mortal wounds, weeping, I gave my soul
> > to Him Who grants forgiveness willingly.'

This was a last-minute choice.

> 'Horrible was the nature of my sins,
> > but boundless mercy stretches out its arms
> > to any man who comes in search of it,'

I'm a pretty bad guy, he says, and I'm lying here dying on this battlefield, and I sincerely, honestly turn to God, and that's all it takes, that's all it takes. It doesn't take the completion of that process. It doesn't take years of bread and water. It takes a word; it takes a gesture. Even if life is escaping you at the moment, this is not, however, about him; it's about the mercy of God. In a sense, this is like all choices; God is ultimately the guide. God offers us this opportunity. I took it.

Herzman: Notice also, he says something here that might seem at first to be a little bit shocking, because remember he is somebody who has been, as Bill said, excommunicated for what he does. Well, what does excommunication mean? He tells us what it doesn't mean. Again, Manfred is still speaking,

'The church's curse is not the final word,
for Everlasting Love may still return,
if hope reveals the slightest hint of green.'

Excommunication is not the Church disposing of your soul in the afterlife. It can't do it; it doesn't have the power to do that, and that's not what it's meant to do. So, even though that excommunication is sort of responsible for Manfred spending a good deal of time here, it has nothing to do with the final disposition of his soul afterwards, and that is another important point that Dante wants to make.

Cook: So, now in the lectures that follow, we're going to begin that journey. It's a struggle at first; it gets easier as we go on toward the gate and then up the Seven-Story Mountain.

Illustrations

Geography of Inferno

Upper Hell

Incontinence
- Vestibule
- 1. Limbo
- 2. Lustful
- 3. Gluttonous
- 4. Hoarders & Wasters
- 5. Wrathful & Slothful

STYX
- City of Dis
- 6. Heresy

Lower Hell

Violence
- 7. The Violent
  - Against Neighbors
  - Against Self
  - Against God

Fraud — Simple
- 8. Fraud (Malebolgia)
  - 1. Panders & Seducers
  - 2. Flatterers
  - 3. Simonists
  - 4. Sorcerers
  - 5. Barrators
  - 6. Hypocrites
  - 7. Thieves
  - 8. Fraudulent Counselors
  - 9. Sowers of Discord
  - 10. Falsifiers

Fraud — Complex
- 9. Treachery (Cocytus)
  - Caina - Traitors to Kin
  - Antenora - Traitors to Country
  - Ptolomea - Traitors to Guests
  - Judecca - Traitors to Lords

Earth's Center

VII. The Lustful

VI. The Gluttonous

V. The Avaricious and Prodigal

IV. The Slothful

III. The Wrathful

II. The Envious

I. The Proud

Gate of Purgatóry

The Negligent, Indolent, Unshriven

The Excommunicated

The Island Of Purgatory

7 Terraces of Purgation

Excessive Love | Deficient Love | Misdirected Love | Late Repentant

PURGATORY PROPER | ANTEPURGATORY

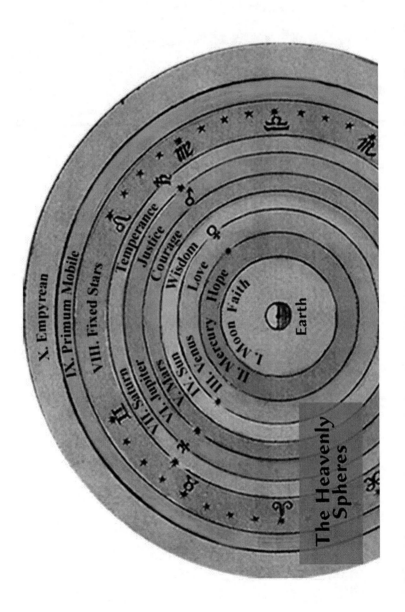

The Heavenly Spheres

1. St. Thomas Aquinas
2. Albertus Magnus
3. Gratian
4. Peter Lombard
5. Solomon
6. Dionysius the Areopagite
7. Orosius
8. Boethius
9. Isidore of Seville
10. Bede
11. Richard of St. Victor
12. Siger of Brabant

Dante   Beatrice

Souls of the
Wise and
Learned

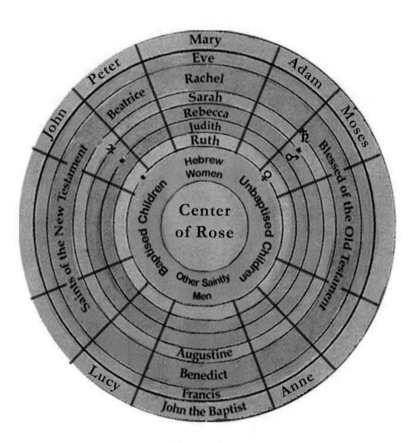

The Celestial Rose

Timeline for the Life of Dante

1265 ....Birth of Dante Alighieri in Florence.

1274 ....Traditionally the year when Dante first saw Beatrice.

c. 1285......................................Marriage of Dante and Gemma Donati.

1289 ....Dante participates in the Battle of Campaldino against Arezzo.

c. 1293–1295.............................Dante writes the *Vita Nuova*, a collection of his earlier love poems with commentary.

1300 ....Dante chosen as a prior of Florence; date of the journey of Dante to the afterlife.

1301 (September)......................Dante in Rome to negotiate with Pope Boniface VIII.

1301 (November)......................Black Guelfs enter Florence.

1302 (January) ....Dante formally condemned and exiled.

1304 ....Dante breaks with his fellow White Guelfs.

1307 (?)–1320/21 ....Dante writes the *Commedia*.

1310s...Dante lives mostly in Verona under the patronage of Can Grande della Scala.

1310–1313.................................Descent of Emperor Henry VII into Italy.

1318–1321.................................Dante lives in Ravenna under the patronage of the da Polenta family.

1321 ....Death of Dante in Ravenna.

Timeline for the Political World of Dante

1215 ....Traditional date for the beginning of serious factionalism in Florence.

1248–1251...................................First Ghibelline rule in Florence.

1250 ....Death of the Emperor Frederick II.

1260 ....Battle of Montaperti.

1260–1266...................................Second Ghibelline rule in Florence (under Farinata degli Uberti).

1266 ....Defeat of Manfred at Benevento.

1268 ....Defeat of Conradin, the last legitimate heir of the Hohenstaufen dynasty) at Tagliacozzo.

1269 ....Defeat of Tuscan Ghibellines at the Battle of Colle Valdelsa (death of Provenzan Salvani).

1280 ....General amnesty for Ghibellines in Florence (degli Uberti family excepted).

1294–1303...................................Pontificate of Boniface VIII.

1299 ....Division of the Florentine Guelfs into Black and White factions.

1301 ....Expulsion of White Guelfs from Florence.

1310–1313...................................Campaign of Emperor Henry VII in Italy.

Timeline for Characters and Events in Dante's *Commedia* in the Lectures*

Thirteenth century B.C.E. .... Supposed date of Trojan War.

46 B.C.E. .... Suicide of Cato (Purgatory 1).

44 B.C.E. .... Murder of Julius Caesar (Brutus and Cassius, Inferno 34).

19 B.C.E. .... Death of Virgil.

33 C.E.. .... Traditional date of Christ's Crucifixion (Judas, Inferno 34) and, thus, of the Harrowing of Hell (Inferno 4).

96 .... Death of Statius (Purgatory 21–28).

117 .... Death of the Emperor Trajan (mentioned in Purgatory 10; Paradise 20).

337 .... Death of the Emperor Constantine (mentioned in Inferno 19; alluded to in Purgatory 32; Paradise 20).

547 .... Death of Saint Benedict (Paradise 22 and 32).

565 .... Death of the Emperor Justinian (Paradise 6).

c. 1150 .... Death of Cacciaguida (Paradise 15–17).

1153 .... Death of Saint Bernard of Clairvaux (Paradise 31–33).

1198 .... Death of Empress Constance (Paradise 3).

1221 .... Death of Saint Dominic (Paradise 12).

1226 .... Death of Saint Francis of Assisi (Paradise 11 and 32).

c. 1248	Suicide of Pier delle Vigne (Inferno 13).
1250	Death of Emperor Frederick II (Inferno 10 and 13); death of Romeo of Villeneuve (Paradise 6).
1259	Death of Omberto Aldobrandesco (Purgatory 11).
1260	Battle of Montaperti (Inferno 10 and 32).
1264	Death of Farinata degli Uberti (Inferno 10).
1266	Death of Manfred at the Battle of Benevento (Purgatory 3).
after 1267(?)	Death of Marco Lombardo (Purgatory 16–18).
1269	Death of Provenzan Salvani at the Battle of Colle Valdelsa (Purgatory 11).
ca. 1269	Death of Sordello (Purgatory 6).
1274	Deaths of Saint Bonaventure (Paradise 12) and Saint Thomas Aquinas (Paradise 11).
1280	Death of Pope Nicholas III (Inferno 19).
ca. 1280	Death of Cavalcante de' Cavalcanti (Inferno 10).
after 1282	Death of Casella (Purgatory 2).
ca. 1285	Murder of Paolo and Francesca (Inferno 5).
1289	Death of Count Ugolino (Inferno 32 and 33); death of Buonconte da Montefeltro at the Battle of Campaldino (Purgatory 5).
1290	Death of Beatrice.

1290s	Death of Piccarda Donati (Paradise 3).
1294	Pontificate of Celestine V (probably the one who made the great refusal, Inferno 3); death of Brunetto Latini (Inferno 15).
1294–1303	Pontificate of Boniface VIII (Inferno 19 and 27).
1295	Death of Archbishop Ruggieri (Inferno 32 and 33).
ca. 1295	Death of Pia de' Tolomei (Purgatory 5).
1296	Death of Forese Donati (Purgatory 33).
1297	Death of Bonagiunta da Lucca (Purgatory 24).
1298	Death of Guido da Montefeltro (Inferno 27).
ca. 1299	Death of Oderisi da Gubbio (Purgatory 11).
1302	Death of Cimabue (mentioned in Purgatory 11).
1313	Death of Emperor Henry VII (mentioned in Paradise 30).
1314	Death of Clement V (mentioned in Inferno 18).
1337	Death of Giotto (mentioned in Purgatory 11).

*This timeline does not include fictional characters (such as Ulysses and Jason) or biblical characters.

Bibliography

Essential Reading:

Anderson, William. *Dante the Maker.* Crossroads, 1982. This work combines extensive information about Dante's life and times with an analysis of all his works. It is useful to someone who wants information about Dante's works other than the *Commedia.*

Augustine. *The Confessions.* Trans. R. S. Pine-Coffin. New York: Penguin Books, 1961. The classic spiritual autobiography that provides a model for the first-person narrative of the *Commedia.* Readers who want a quick course in the *Confessions* as it would be useful for a reading of Dante might concentrate on Books 7 and 8. Book 7 is Augustine's encounter with the Platonist philosophers. Book 8 is the actual conversion of Augustine.

Bemrose, Stephen. *A New Life of Dante.* Exeter: University of Exeter Press, 2000. The most modern biography of Dante in English. A chronological examination of the life of Dante with a good deal of historical analysis of Dante's literary and philosophical works. This book is useful for those who want to know the story of the poet's life and the historical conditions in which he composed his major works.

The Bible. (Any good modern edition will do, though readers should be aware that some differences exist between the Latin Vulgate Bible that Dante knew and modern editions. The Douay-Rheims version in English is a translation of the Vulgate text, though for most purposes such precision is not necessary.) The Bible is the most important "source" for Dante, and serious readers of his poem will find themselves routinely looking up biblical passages. To those who are unfamiliar with the Bible, a reading of Genesis; Exodus; some Psalms; some chapters from Prophets, such as Isaiah and Jeremiah; at least one synoptic Gospel (that is, either Matthew, Mark, or Luke); the Gospel of John; and Paul's Epistle to the Romans would be a good starting point.

Cook, William R., and Ronald B. Herzman. *The Medieval World View.* New York: Oxford University Press, 1983 (Second edition forthcoming.) Chapters on biblical and classical influences on the Middle Ages, as well as on medieval institutions and politics, make this a very useful companion for first-time readers of Dante.

Dante. *The Divine Comedy.* Ed. and Trans. Charles S. Singleton. Princeton: Princeton University Press, 1970–75. This six-volume set is the standard edition for English readers, with facing-page Italian and English translation. Singleton's translation is literal and his commentary, a huge volume for each of the three parts of the poem, is extremely detailed. One of the problems for first-time readers of Dante is that the commentary can be somewhat overwhelming, because it is directed more to scholars than to the general reader.

————. *The Divine Comedy*. Trans. Mark Musa. New York: Penguin, 1971–84. A useful edition because Musa's notes are often thorough but also accessible to the general reader.

————. *The Divine Comedy*. Trans. Allen Mandelbaum. New York: Bantam Books, 1980–86. An inexpensive facing-page Italian/English edition of the poem, Mandelbaum's version is useful, although his notes are not as complete or as user friendly as those of other editions.

————. *Dante's Vita Nuova*. Trans. Mark Musa. Bloomington: Indiana University Press, 1973. A treatise on the nature of love, this early work (the title means "the new life") would be extremely important even apart from its account of Dante's love for Beatrice, who is his second guide in the *Commedia*. It consists of beautiful lyric poems connected by a commentary that makes the work a kind of poetic autobiography.

————. *Dante, "Monarchia."* Trans. Prue Shaw. Cambridge: Cambridge University Press, 1995. Dante's treatise on government, this work is a significant contribution to political theory

Dante Studies. The journal published annually by the Dante Society of America, it includes critical articles on Dante and an annotated bibliography of works published on Dante in English during the previous year. The journal is sent to members of the Dante Society of America, which was founded by Henry Wadsworth Longfellow. The society is not limited to Dante scholars but is open to anyone with an interest in Dante.

Freccero, John. *Dante: The Poetics of Conversion*. Ed. Rachel Jacoff. Cambridge: Harvard University Press, 1986. A collection of essays written over a period of many years by one of the most influential modern American critics. As the title indicates, Freccero's emphasis is on the nature of the poem as the conversion experience of Dante the pilgrim.

Hollander, Robert. *Allegory in Dante's Commedia*. Princeton: Princeton University Press, 1969. This is a standard treatment of allegory as it is used by Dante in the *Commedia*, in which Hollander makes important and useful distinctions between the "allegory of the poets" and the "allegory of the theologians."

Jacoff, Rachel, ed. *The Cambridge Companion to Dante*. Cambridge: Cambridge University Press, 1993. This volume contains individual essays on Dante's life and times; the political, historical, and theological background of the *Commedia*; and Dante's works, including the *Commedia*. An extremely useful volume, the *CCD* is a valuable entry point into the world of Dante scholarship.

Lansing, Richard, ed. *The Dante Encyclopedia*. New York: Garland, 2000. A major new source in English for Dante and subjects related to him, as well as for bibliographical information (each article ends with a brief bibliography). This work is an excellent "first stop" for readers of the *Comedy*, with hundreds of articles summarizing recent scholarship and the scholarly tradition. The work is wide ranging in its approach; articles even include such subjects as Dante in the cinema, as well as the major figures named in the poem and such topics as allegory, apocalypticism, mendicant orders, and so on.

Ovid. *Metamorphoses*. Trans. Mary Innes. New York: Penguin, 1955. Dante draws heavily on the *Metamorphoses*, especially in Paradise. Next to the *Aeneid*, it is the most frequently quoted work from the classical tradition in the *Comedy*. Readers not familiar with the text might want to begin with the stories of Arachne, Procne and Tereus, and Jason and Medea, all of which are central to the *Comedy*.

Virgil. *The Aeneid of Virgil*. Trans. Allen Mandelbaum. New York: Bantam Books, 1961. A convenient edition of the great epic written by Dante's first guide to the afterlife. Dante expects his readers to have a working knowledge of the *Aeneid*. The more the reader knows of Virgil, the richer Dante's poem becomes. For readers who do not know the poem, a quick course to prepare for reading Dante should include Book 2, the Fall of Troy; Book 4, the story of Aeneas and Dido; and Book 6, Aeneas's trip to the underworld.

www.princeton.edu/~dante. Readers of Dante's *Comedy* should know that his poem has successfully made the transition to the computer age. This Web site presents a multimedia edition of the poem, as well as connections to a number of other important Dante sites, including the Dartmouth Dante Project, an on-line edition of important Dante commentaries in all languages from Dante's time until the twentieth century. (Some fifty-nine commentaries are currently on line.) This site offers access to important bibliographic material and to other sites that deal with Dante, including foreign sites. Any reader of the poem would do well to spend some time browsing here.

Supplementary Reading:

Auerbach, Erich. *Mimesis: The Representation of Reality in Western Literature.* Trans. Willard Trask. New York: Doubleday, 1957. An extremely influential work of literary criticism. Auerbach's chapter on "Farinata and Cavalcante" is a classic.

Barolini, Teodolinda. *Dante's Poets: Textuality and Truth in the Commedia.* Princeton: Princeton University Press, 1984. This work shows how Dante appropriates earlier poets in both the vernacular and the classical traditions in the *Commedia.*

Bloom, Harold, ed. *Modern Critical Views: Dante.* New York: Chelsea House, 1986. A collection of some of the most famous articles published on Dante and his *Commedia.* A good sampler of Dante scholarship in the English-speaking world.

Boase, T. S. R. *Boniface VIII.* London: Constable & Co., 1933. The standard biography of Dante's nemesis, Pope Boniface VIII, in English. Learning about Boniface is valuable for understanding all three parts of the *Commedia.*

Bonaventure. *The Soul's Journey into God, The Tree of Life, The Life of St. Francis.* Trans. and ed. Ewert Cousins. Mahwah, NJ: Paulist Press, 1978. *The Life of St. Francis* by Bonaventure is the major source for the story of Francis in Paradiso 11. *The Soul's Journey into God* is one of the most important mystical treatises of the Middle Ages and greatly influences the entire structure of the Paradiso.

Bornstein, Daniel L., trans. *Dino Compagni's Chronicle of Florence.* Philadelphia: University of Pennsylvania Press, 1986. This chronicle was written by a contemporary of Dante's, who was also a member of the same White Guelf Party as Dante was. It provides a look at the turbulent world Dante describes from a contemporary perspective. The introduction gives useful background information.

Boyde, Patrick. *Dante, Philomythes and Philosopher: Man in the Cosmos.* Cambridge: Cambridge University Press, 1981. A comprehensive treatment of Dante in relation to scientific subjects.

Brandeis, Irma. *The Ladder of Vision.* New York: Doubleday, 1962. A short but helpful book for learning how to read Dante.

Cachey, Theodore J., Jr. *Dante Now: Current Trends in Dante Studies*. Notre Dame, IN: University of Notre Dame Press, 1995. Essays on a wide variety of topics, extending all the way to an essay on Dante in the "Video Decade."

Cassell, Anthony K. *Lectura Dantis Americana: Inferno I*. Philadelphia: University of Pennsylvania Press, 1989. The first volume in a series commissioned by the Dante Society of America. Each volume is to be devoted to a single canto of the poem.

Cavalcanti, Guido. *The Complete Poems*. Trans. Marc Cirigliano. New York: Italica Press, 1992. A dual-language edition of the poems of Dante's friend and fellow Florentine poet, who figures prominently in the *Commedia*.

Charity, A. C. *Events and Their Afterlife*. Cambridge: Cambridge University Press, 1966. A study of Christian typology in itself and as it related to Dante.

Cogan, Marc. *The Design in the Wax*. Notre Dame, IN: University of Notre Dame Press, 1999. Examines each of the three canticles of the *Commedia* from the perspective of Dante's use and interpretation of Aristotle and medieval Aristotelians.

Dante. *Il Convivio (The Banquet)*. Trans. Richard Lansing. New York: Garland, 1990. A philosophical work that Dante left unfinished, many believe, when he began to write the *Commedia*.

———. *The Divine Comedy*. Trans. John Ciardi. New York: Norton, 1970. Ciardi's translation is frequently used as a school text. Ciardi is a poet rather than a Dante scholar, and his translation reflects that approach.

———. *The Divine Comedy*. Trans. Dorothy L. Sayers. Baltimore: Penguin, 1949–52. Sayers (and Barbara Reynolds, who completed the translation of the last cantos of the Paradiso after the death of Sayers) undertook the somewhat quixotic task of translating Dante's *terza rima* into English *terza rima*. Almost all words in Italian end in vowels, thus greatly expanding the possibilities for rhyme. Because of a lack of rhyme words in English, the translation appears strained and "Victorian" to most readers, although it does have its admirers. More important are Sayers's introductions and notes, which are especially interesting and useful with respect to matters of dogma. See, for example, her discussion of the doctrine of purgatory in the introduction to that volume. The diagrams in this edition are also important and have been used for later editions, such as Musa.

———. *The Inferno*. Trans. Robert Hollander and Jean Hollander. Introduction and notes by Robert Hollander. New York: Doubleday, 2000. The newest translation of the Inferno, with facing-page Italian, this volume contains an extensive bibliography and elaborate notes. The expectation is that the other two volumes of the *Commedia* will be published relatively soon, at which time this will become an important English edition of the entire poem. The notes are somewhat less formidable than those of Singleton and somewhat more formidable than those of Musa. Many of Hollander's notes take into account the extensive commentary tradition associated with the poem.

———. *The Divine Comedy of Dante Alighieri: Inferno*. Ed. and trans. Robert M. Durling. Introduction and notes by Ronald Martinez and Robert M. Durling. New York and Oxford: Oxford University Press, 1995. Another important recent translation, with facing-page Italian. The other volumes are scheduled to be published soon. One feature of this edition is that it includes "additional notes," short essays on a variety of topics at the end of the volume.

———. *The Literary Criticism of Dante Alighieri*. Trans. and ed. Robert S. Haller. Lincoln: University of Nebraska Press, 1973. Contains a translation of Dante's Letter to Can Grande, and the text of "*De Vulgari Eloquentia*," his treatise on the necessity of writing in the vernacular.

Davis, Charles T. *Dante and the Idea of Rome*. Oxford: Oxford University Press, 1957. Standard study of Dante in relation to classical political thought.

———. *Dante's Italy and Other Essays*. Philadelphia: University of Pennsylvania Press, 1984. A collection of essays on Italian and particularly Florentine politics relevant to Dante.

Emmerson, Richard K., and Ronald B. Herzman. *The Apocalyptic Imagination in Medieval Literature*. Philadelphia: University of Pennsylvania Press, 1992. This book contains a chapter on Dante and the apocalyptic imagination. Understanding apocalypticism is especially important for an understanding of the ending of Purgatory.

Ferrante, Joan. *The Political Vision of the Divine Comedy*. Princeton: Princeton University Press, 1984. A reading of the poem through the filter of political concerns, this work has a good deal of useful information on the political aspects of the *Commedia*.

Gardiner, Eileen, ed. *Visions of Heaven and Hell Before Dante.* New York: Italica Press, 1989. A collection of twelve of the most influential visions of heaven and hell written before Dante.

Giamatti, A. Bartlett, ed. *Dante in America: The First Two Centuries.* Binghamton, NY: Medieval and Renaissance Texts and Studies, 1983. A collection of American essays about Dante. This book includes works by Henry Wadsworth Longfellow, James Russell Lowell, George Santayana, Ezra Pound, and T. S. Eliot, as well as some of the greatest American Dantists.

Gilson, Etienne. *Dante and Philosophy.* Trans. David Moore. London: Sheed & Ward, 1949. A justifiably famous study of the philosophy of the *Commedia* by one of the great scholars of the twentieth century.

Hawkins, Peter. *Dante's Testaments.* Stanford: Stanford University Press, 1999. A work of criticism done with an emphasis on the personal as well as the scholarly. The chapters in this work deal mostly with aspects of Dante's relationship to the Bible.

Jacoff, Rachel, and Jeffrey T. Schnapp. *The Poetry of Allusion: Virgil and Ovid in Dante's Commedia.* Stanford: Stanford University Press, 1991. This collection of essays shows how, by specific textual readings, these two great classical poets inform Dante's work. These essays offer good examples of how Dante works "intertextually."

Jacoff, Rachel, and William A. Stephany. *Lectura Dantis Americana: Inferno II.* Philadelphia: University of Pennsylvania Press, 1989. This second volume in the series is particularly informative with respect to the role of Saint Paul in the poem.

Jones, Philip. *The Italian City-State: From Commune to Signoria.* Oxford: Clarendon Press, 1997. A detailed and often hard-to-read book, but it is the most thorough concerning the political and economic milieu in which Dante lived and about which he wrote. A book to be consulted more than read.

Kirkpatrick, Robin. *Dante's Inferno: Difficulty and Dead Poetry.* Cambridge: Cambridge University Press, 1987. A canto-by-canto reading of Inferno. The author stresses the relationship of Inferno to the other two canticles and argues that readers need to recognize the tensions in the poem rather than seeing it as neat and consistent in every detail.

Maginnis, Hayden B. J. *Painting in the Age of Giotto: A Historical Reevaluation.* State College, PA: The Pennsylvania State University

Press, 1997. A modern study of Italian art in the age of Giotto, an almost exact Florentine contemporary of Dante and as revolutionary in the art of painting as Dante was in poetry.

Mazzotta, Giuseppe. *Dante: Poet of the Desert.* Princeton: Princeton University Press, 1979. This work shows how Virgil, and the classical world in general, was read by Augustine and by Dante and describes Dante's more "optimistic" take on his encounter with the classical world.

Moleta, Vincent. *From St. Francis to Giotto.* Chicago: Franciscan Herald Press (now Quincy, IL: Franciscan Press), 1983. An accessible introduction to the development of Franciscan spirituality and Italian art in the thirteenth century. It includes a chapter on Francis in the *Commedia.*

Musa, Mark. *Advent at the Gates: Dante's* Comedy. Bloomington: Indiana University Press, 1974. A close reading of several cantos of Inferno and Purgatorio by one of the most distinguished modern translators of Dante.

Norwich, John Julius. *The Normans in Sicily.* London: Penguin Books, 1967, 1970. This edition combines Norwich's two volumes on Sicily in the time before Dante. This work provides a great deal of important background for material that finds its way into the poem.

Parker, Deborah. *Commentary and Ideology: Dante in the Renaissance.* Durham and London: Duke University Press, 1993. This work shows how Dante was read in the Renaissance. Equally important, it is a good introduction to the commentary tradition on Dante.

Royal, Robert. *Dante Alighieri:* Divine Comedy, *Divine Spirituality.* New York: Crossroad, 1999. An examination of the *Commedia* and each of its three canticles as a work of Christian spirituality.

Ruggiers, Paul G. *Florence in the Age of Dante.* Norman, OK: University of Oklahoma Press, 1964. A rather short, general account of Florentine history at the time of Dante. Written for a general audience, it is an easy entry into the world in which Dante lived.

Runciman, Steven. *The Sicilian Vespers.* Cambridge: Cambridge University Press, 1958. This work uses the famous revolt in Sicily in 1282 as the focus for a history of the Mediterranean world in the later thirteenth century. This is the very history that Dante is implicated in and one of the great subjects for his poem.

Russell, Jeffrey Burton. *A History of Heaven.* Princeton: Princeton University Press, 1997. One of the last chapters of this study is explicitly on Dante's Paradiso, but the book is more generally valuable to students of Dante by showing how heaven has been imagined and pictured throughout Christian history.

Schnapp, Jeffrey. *The Transfiguration of History at the Center of Dante's Paradise.* Princeton: Princeton University Press, 1986. Sophisticated and perceptive reading of the Circle of Mars in Paradise.

Scott, John A. *Dante's Political Purgatory.* Philadelphia: University of Pennsylvania Press, 1996. Argues that politics plays as important a part in purgatory as it does in the other sections of the afterlife.

Thompson, David. *Dante's Epic Journeys.* Baltimore: Johns Hopkins University Press, 1974. A short book that focuses on Dante's creative uses of the stories of Ulysses and Aeneas as they were known and understood in the Middle Ages.

Waley, Daniel. *The Italian City Republics.* New York: McGraw Hill, 1960. A good introductory historical study of Dante's world. Waley's maps and charts are also useful.

Notes

Notes